KIERKEGAARD AND BULTMANN:

THE QUEST

OF THE

HISTORICAL JESUS

An Augsburg Publishing House Theological Monograph

BY HERBERT C. WOLF

AUGSBURG PUBLISHING HOUSE
MINNEAPOLIS, MINNESOTA

KIERKEGAARD AND BULTMANN:
THE QUEST OF THE HISTORICAL JESUS

Acknowledgments of permission to quote from copyrighted
works are indicated in footnotes on pages 93 ff.

KIERKEGAARD AND BULTMANN:
THE QUEST
OF THE
HISTORICAL
JESUS

Preface

Kierkegaard knew too well that he was leaving no little capital to that inheritor of all good things, the professor. (In fact, with typical irony he expected that even this awareness on his part would probably some day find its place in a lecture or even a preface!) Strangely, however, one aspect of Kierkegaard's legacy which has remained relatively untouched is his understanding of the Bible.

In this monograph I have turned to a particular aspect of Kierkegaard's biblical thought, his understanding of the historical Jesus. My personal interest in this subject is two-fold. First, it corresponds to a continuing and growing concern in contemporary Christian thought regarding that subject which serves as the juncture between (or the foundation beneath) biblical studies and theology, i.e., hermeneutics. Secondly, in the discussion regarding faith and the historical Jesus and the documents concerning him, Kierkegaard's contributions continue to provide fuel for the fire—and light and warmth as well.

This is not to suggest that Kierkegaard is to be elevated to some semi-apostolic authority (as some would do) to be heeded and adhered to in subsequent generations. He perceived himself as a "corrective" in his own age, pointing men from "the System" to the Crucified One. Others must perform comparable tasks in their age. This Bultmann has done by radically reaffirming the centrality of the proclamation of the kerygma in categories which communicate to and challenge modern man. Hence the discussion of Bultmann naturally evolved out of that of Kierkegaard, and the correspondence and difference between the two will become apparent.

The intent of this discussion is not to solve the hermeneutical problem once and for all—or even for our age! It is to raise again the vexing problem of the relationship of faith to the historical Jesus and to provoke a consideration of some fundamental matters in the life of faith by a critical examination of the thought of two theologians, both of whom are too readily accepted or rejected today.

Perhaps the temptation to quote extensively from Kierkegaard's writings has been succumbed to a bit too often, and many times phrases have been lifted from his works and included in the discussion. These things have been done in a deliberate attempt to give something of Kierkegaard's distinctive flavor to the first part of the book. The number of references is not, therefore, intended to be pedantry, but is simply a means of making accessible more of Kierkegaard's colorful and incisive language on this subject than is available in the relatively limited indexes to his works

Finally, in both sections of the monograph I have essentially confined myself to my understanding of the primary sources in preference to the interpretations of the commonly accepted critics. At least these have stimulated Bultmann to more precise and extended statements of his position; but, as in the case of Kierkegaard, there is no little difference of opinion among them as to what he is saying.

HERBERT C. WOLF

Table of Contents

Introduction

At first sight there would seem to be a confusion of categories, or at least an anachronistic element, in a title combining Kierkegaard and "the quest of the historical Jesus." Kierkegaard was not interested in the attempts of scholars at reconstructing a life of Jesus which would give some sense of historical assurance to one's faith in Christ. As we shall note in considerable detail later, his concern lay elsewhere. His categories were existential, not historical. Secondly, in spite of the fact that he lived at the juncture of the two periods into which Schweitzer divides the nineteenth-century quest ("before Strauss . . . after Strauss"[1]), Kierkegaard receives no notice in Schweitzer's extensive survey. The reasons for this omission may be many; but the very omission itself points to one obvious aspect of the phenomenon of Kierkegaard—the discovery of his relevance above all in and to the twentieth century.

In order to correlate these two apparently divergent subjects, Kierkegaard and the quest of the historical Jesus, and to expand them to include Bultmann, we must first briefly clarify the various meanings implicit in the phrase "the historical Jesus." One use of this term would make it synonymous with Jesus of Nazareth as he "actually lived" in the midst of his contemporaries in Palestine, "as if the adjective 'historical' were a meaningless addition."[2] Through-

9

out most of the life of the church, even in the twentieth century, the "greatest story ever told" has been assumed to be a
relatively simple possibility. By scissors and paste one could
harmonize the four or at least three Gospels, insert a bit of
noncanonical tradition and imaginative detail where helpful
or necessary, and the result would be an account of Jesus
Christ, God incarnate. The theological presuppositions are
all too apparent in the "historical" conclusions.

With the advent of the Enlightenment, a new sense of the
historical, freed from supernatural dogma and control, made
it possible to conceive a new understanding of Jesus. He was,
in Schweitzer's phrase, no longer "like Lazarus of old bound
hand and foot with grave-clothes—the grave-clothes of the
dogma of the Dual Nature."[3] This approach to the historical
Jesus maintained that Jesus of Nazareth could be properly
discovered only by means of the scientific method of the
historian. *Historie* was "the subject matter of historical
science, which seeks to divest itself of all presuppositions
and prejudices and to establish objective facts."[4] The historical Jesus of Nazareth was identified with the historical
"facts" of Jesus' life as reconstructed by a positivistic historiography, emancipated from theological presuppositions.

The inadequacy of this nineteenth-century view of "objectivity" was soon apparent, particularly as it sought in vain
to contain the deeper level of meaning identified with Jesus
of Nazareth. Schweitzer spoke the eulogy at the graveside
of the nineteenth-century historiographical approach to Jesus in words which, despite many divergences, have an
astonishingly Kierkegaardian ring about them:

> There is nothing more negative than the result of the critical study
> of the Life of Jesus. . . . Jesus means something to our world because
> a mighty spiritual force streams forth from Him and flows through
> our time also. This fact can neither be shaken nor confirmed by any
> historical discovery. It is the solid foundation of Christianity. . . .
> "If we have known Christ after the flesh yet henceforth we know
> Him no more." . . . And further we must be prepared to find that the

historical knowledge of the personality and life of Jesus will not be a help, but perhaps even an offence to religion. . . . It is not given to history to disengage that which is abiding and eternal in the being of Jesus. . . . The abiding and eternal in Jesus is absolutely independent of historical knowledge. . . . In proportion as we have the Spirit of Jesus we have the true knowledge of Jesus. . . . He comes to us as One unknown, without a name, as of old, by the lake-side, He came to those men who knew Him not. He speaks to us the same word: "Follow thou me!" and sets us to the tasks which He has to fulfil for our time. He commands. And to those who obey Him, whether they be wise or simple, He will reveal Himself in the toils, the conflicts, the sufferings which they shall pass through in His fellowship, and, as an ineffable mystery, they shall learn in their own experience Who He is.[5]

Subsequent studies of the literary forms of the Gospel sources (Formgeschichte) ascertained their Sitz im Leben within the early church which was responsible for both their creation and preservation. At the same time there came a new appreciation of the centrality of the kerygma, or oral proclamation, of the New Testament community. These developments implied both "the impossibility and illegitimacy"[6] of the quest for historicity on both levels proposed above. The consequence of this has been a certain embarrassment, or at least uneasiness, regarding the relationship between the biblical records and faith today, particularly with respect to historical facticity concerning Jesus himself.

The hermeneutics of the mid-twentieth century is confronted simultaneously with the absence of certainty regarding the historical facts of Jesus' life and early Christianity, and with the acknowledgment of the indispensability of historical events for the Christian faith. The new attempts to deal with this dilemma are varied. They are represented by Bultmann and demythologizing, the "new quest" (Fuchs, Bornkamm, James M. Robinson, etc.), Richard R. Niebuhr and the concern to establish an independent historical reason, and Dodd and Cullmann and the stress on Heilsgeschichte. But in all of them, the distinctively new feature . . . is an attempt on the part of its exponents to come to grips with the nature of historical fact or historical event. These critics are keenly aware with Kierkegaard of the paradox of purporting to find a doctrine of absolute importance in an historical event that does not admit of demonstrative proof. . . . The attempt, in short, is to develop a new self-consciousness that will enable theology confidently to expound doctrine, doctrine, moreover, that is based only on probable, i.e., historical events. The intent . . . is to avoid two common perils. The first is the obvious one of sacrificing the integrity of historical critical reason. . . . The second . . . is the danger of discounting too readily the historical character of parts of the New Testament.[7]

This quotation brings us explicitly to Kierkegaard and the quest of the historical Jesus. It has already been noted that Schweitzer makes no mention of Kierkegaard in his discussion of the nineteenth-century quest. Similarly, histories of hermeneutics in that century ignore him, and biblical expositors essentially bypass his contributions to exegesis. Even relatively contemporary discussions of his theology indicate little interest in his role as a biblical interpreter.* Theology, since the days of Barth's Römerbrief, has not been able to avoid the influence of Kierkegaard. Biblical studies, on the other hand, have only slowly recognized the necessity of dealing with his hermeneutics as well as his theological categories. "Histories of twentieth-century hermeneutics, unlike those of the nineteenth, will be quite unable to ignore the influence of this 'genius in a market town.' "[8]

In the first part of this study we shall approach Kierkegaard and the quest of the historical Jesus from two directions. First, we shall seek to show something of his attitude towards the Jesus of history in the first sense suggested above: Jesus as he actually lived in Galilee and Judea nineteen centuries ago. This will be ascertained primarily by an analysis of some of Kierkegaard's references and allusions to the life of Jesus. As an introduction to this, some mention must be

---

* See, for example, Types of Modern Theology, by H. R. Mackintosh.

made of his general attitude towards the Bible. Also we must note his reaction to the growing science of biblical criticism and the quest of the historical Jesus in the second sense suggested above, as well as his response to the antithesis of that quest as implicit in the orthodoxy of the Danish Lutheran Church.

Secondly, we shall deal more thoroughly with Kierkegaard's understanding of the historical Jesus in connection with the question he poses through Johannes Climacus as the subtitle to *Philosophical Fragments:* "Is an historical point of departure possible for an eternal consciousness; how can such a point of departure have any other than a merely historical interest; is it possible to base an eternal happiness upon historical knowledge?"[9] Here we come directly to that aspect of Kierkegaard's hermeneutics which is of such importance in both contemporary theology and biblical studies —an existential relationship of faith to the historical Jesus. In effect, this constitutes a third aspect of the phrase "the historical Jesus."

The second part of this book will examine the possible influence which Kierkegaard's hermeneutics may have had on that of Bultmann. This is not to suggest that so creative a theologian as Bultmann is dependent upon Kierkegaard— or upon Kierkegaard alone! He readily acknowledges his debt to Kierkegaard, as well as to Wrede, Weiss, Herrmann, and others. But Bultmann utilizes their insights in his own way to face a mid-twentieth-century version of a problem remarkably similar to that faced a century earlier by Kierkegaard: How is faith related to historically uncertain facts? The aim of this section will be to note how Bultmann deals with this problem in the context of the earlier presentation of Kierkegaard's approach. The intent, therefore, is not to describe all of Bultmann's thought, but only some of those points which by comparison or contrast appear to be related to Kierkegaard's discussion of the subject.

Part I

Kierkegaard
and the
Quest
of the
Historical
Jesus

I. The Historical Jesus

"The Bible is always on my table and is the book I read most."[10] This confession of Victor Eremita is equally that of the creator of the pseudonym. Any superficial reading of Kierkegaard's works, even those written pseudonymously in the esthetic sphere of existence, will produce sufficient evidence to indicate his profound familiarity with the biblical text. A broader reading must lead into the works intended for edification, in which biblical texts constitute the springboard for discussions not necessarily related to the Christian faith but intended to induce religious inwardness. But a deeper reading of Kierkegaard will indicate that everywhere his thought, and even his vocabulary, is colored by biblical imagery and phraseology—a certain sign of the intimacy of his encounter with the Bible.* It is strange, however, that a survey of books and periodicals on Kierkegaard shows that little has been written about the influence of the Bible on his thought.

While our concern is not explicitly with Kierkegaard's use of the Bible, it is relevant to our purposes to note the existential character of his understanding of the Scriptures. "A ma-

---

*Kierkegaard and the Bible, an Index, by Paul S. Minear and Paul S. Morimoto, Princeton Theological Seminary, 1953, consists of 19 double-columned pages classifying references which are conscious and explicit expositions of biblical texts or, more frequently, brief citations and allusions, sometimes intentional, often spontaneous, in their use of the Bible.

ture person learns only by appropriation, and he appropriates essentially only that which is essential to living."[11] Constantine Constantius, like Victor Eremita, cannot live without the Bible:

> If I had not Job! It is impossible to describe and to *nuancer* what significance he has for me, and how manifold his significance is. I do not read him as one reads another book with the eye, but I read this book as it were with my heart, with the eye of the heart I read it. . . . Every word of his is food and gladness and medicine for my ailing soul. Now one word rouses me from my lethargy, . . . now it quiets the fruitless fury within me. . . . Although I have read the book again and again, every word is new to me. . . . These words I make my own.[12]

There are always those esthetic spectators who develop that "certain disingeniousness of spirit, which seeks to protect itself . . . by means of admiration." The message of the text then

> degenerates into a matter for discussion and critical examination pro and con; the communication is twisted and turned on every side, to see whether, now really, etc. . . . Job's faith should be so presented that it becomes a challenge, a question directed to me, as to whether I do desire to acquire a believing mind. By no means should it be permitted to signify that I have an invitation to become a spectator at a comedy, or to play the role of a member of a public investigating whether now actually, or applauding that now really.[13]

Similarly, pharisees, sophists, hair-splitters, and dialecticians try to keep their distance from Christ and from doing the truth by asking evasive questions: What is truth? Who is my neighbor? Such persons must be reminded "that Christ took the questioner captive in the answer" and made the questioners (and any who repeat the answer indifferently) responsible to perform the task of love.

> It is infinitely important, that it is Christ who has said it, and that it is said to an individual, it is precisely to *him* that it is said, the whole eternal emphasis is on that *him*, even if in a way it is said to all individuals. . . . The divine authority . . . first compels the accused

to see with whom he is talking, and then it fixes its piercing glance upon him and with this glance it says: "It is you to whom this is said."[14]

Imagine a lover who has received a letter from his beloved.[15] So it is with God's Word. The "learned preliminary work" of translation is merely a necessary evil to get to reading and doing the beloved's will. The lover does not "sit down first and ponder over the obscure passages"[16] with learned commentaries. Rather he complies at once with a single passage that he may be able to understand. Therefore, says Kierkegaard,

> See yourself in the mirror, when you read God's Word. . . . Remember to say to yourself incessantly: "It is talking to me; I am the one it is speaking about." . . . If only you keep on reading God's Word in this manner, sometime you will read a fear and trembling into your soul, and, by God's help, you will succeed in becoming a man, a personality. You will be saved from this horrible nonentity into which we human beings—created in God's image!—have been bewitched, an impersonal, objective something.[17]

It is this existential interpretation of the Bible which determines Kierkegaard's approach to his readers. Imitating the direct personal discourse of "the Pattern" (Jesus), Kierkegaard addresses "my hearer,* thou to whom my discourse is addressed."[18] By empathy, exhortation, and entreaty he seeks the response of "the individual" to the Inviter. "Everything that is Christian must bear some resemblance to the address which a physician makes beside the sickbed."[19] Everything is to be devoted to the single task of "becoming a Christian."

---

*"I understand what is said as addressed solely to me" (i.e., to Kierkegaard first of all). In the "Editor's Preface" to each of the parts of *Training in Christianity*, Kierkegaard admits that "the requirement for being a Christian is strained by the pseudonym to the highest pitch of ideality" so that he himself must "learn not only to take refuge in 'grace,' but to take refuge in such a way as to make use of 'grace'" (p. 7).

The influence of existential methodology in theology and biblical studies today (largely derivative from Kierkegaard in spirit if not in fact) makes it possible that statements such as these need not imply a "conservative" attitude toward the Bible. Such could hardly have been the case in Kierkegaard's day, however. The influence of Danish piety and Lutheran orthodoxy in the Church of Denmark and in Kierkegaard's own life could hardly permit a middle ground between a traditional approach to the Bible and that of the radical scholars of the day, such as Paulus and Strauss. Kierkegaard sought a new place to stand, however, and ultimately rendered useless the oversimplified categories "conservative" and "liberal" regarding biblical criticism today.

In his approach to the historical Jesus, Kierkegaard reflects the traditional understanding of the life of Jesus—the historical Jesus in the first sense described above. But his utilization of this understanding inevitably reflects his own personal predisposition rather than the presuppositions of orthodoxy. A survey of his commentaries and allusions regarding some of the events in the life of Jesus will clarify this.

Kierkegaard assumes the orthodox doctrine that the prophets predicted both the coming of Christ and his sufferings and death. The fact of prophecy, however, is rejected by him as a "proof" for the truth of Christianity. Rather, the inability of Jesus' contemporaries to recognize him as the one "whom the words of the prophets fitted perfectly"[20] is illustrative of the perennial failure of man to understand objectively what he has not personally apprehended. So also with the miracles. Kierkegaard affirms their literal reality as recorded in all four Gospels. This is the case not only with the healing miracles but even more explicitly with the more problematical nature miracles: the feeding of the five thousand, Jesus and Peter walking on the water,[21] changing water into wine, calming the sea,[22] etc. But again, these are not proofs of the deity of Christ (as we shall note later), but related to "the offense."

Blessed is he who is not offended but believes that He fed five thousand men with five loaves and two small fishes; blessed is he who is not offended but believes that this occurred, is not offended because it does not now occur but believes that it occurred. And whatever a man's fate may be in the world, however the storms of life may threaten him—blessed is he who is not offended but believes fully and firmly that Peter sank for the one and only cause that he did not believe fully and firmly. And whatever a man's fault may be, though his guilt were so great that not he himself only but the human race despair of his forgiveness—yet blessed is he who is not offended but believes that He said to the man sick of the palsy, "Thy sins are forgiven thee," and that this was just as easy for Him to say as to say to the palsied man, "Take up thy bed and walk"—blessed is he who is not offended but believes in the forgiveness of sinners, although they are not helped like the palsied man to believe by the certainty of healing. And whatever be the manner of a man's death when his last hour is come— blessed is he who is not offended like the contemporaries when He said, "The damsel is not dead but sleepeth," blessed is he who is not offended but believes, who (like a child who is taught to say these words as it falls asleep) says, "I believe" . . . and then sleeps; yea, blessed is he, he is not dead, he sleepeth.[23]

This uniquely Kierkegaardian approach to the Scriptures can be demonstrated more fully with respect to other events in Jesus' life. Kierkegaard readily conflates the accounts of the four Gospels concerning John the Baptist.[24] He raises no question regarding the facticity of the preaching and the accuracy of the recording of the Beatitudes and the Sermon on the Mount.[25] His memorable discourses on the events of the Passion story, especially the "Discourses at the Communion on Fridays," reveal no reservations regarding the historical reliability of those accounts.[26] As an exegete, he can turn to the literal word of the Greek text against both the critic and the "tasteful explanation" of the "pious and kindly exegete, who by abating the price thought he could smuggle Christianity into the world"[27] by explaining it away or ignoring the hard sayings of Jesus.

> The biblical interpretation of mediocrity goes on interpreting and interprets Christ's words until it gets out of them its own spiritless (trivial) meaning—and then, after having removed all difficulties, it is tranquilized, and appeals confidently to Christ's words! It quite escapes the attention of mediocrity that hereby it generates a new difficulty, surely the most comical difficulty it is possible to imagine, that God should let himself be *born*, that the Truth should have come into the world . . . in order to make trivial remarks.[28]

In contemporary biblical studies, some of the passages most resistant to adequate interpretation in the biblical accounts of the life of Jesus are those of the resurrection and the ascension. There is some indication that Kierkegaard was aware of the problems implicit in these records. His references to the resurrection are infrequent. In the discourse on death in *Thoughts on Crucial Situations,* no suggestion of the resurrection is made; but in this instance the reality of death as an ethical concern is held before his reader, so the omission is understandable.* That the resurrection was affirmed by Kierkegaard is without doubt; but his references to it typically appear most often in contexts which are relevant to his own needs rather than in biblical exposition per se. For example, "Life can be only explained after it has been lived, just as Christ only began to interpret the Scriptures to show how they applied to him—after His resurrection."[29] In his discussion of the raising of Lazarus in the Introduction to *The Sickness unto Death,* Kierkegaard assumes the reality of that miracle and alludes to Christ as "the resurrection and the life"; but no reference is made to Christ's own resurrection, except indirectly:

---

*This existential focusing upon death may be related to Kierkegaard's ready acceptance and use of the traditional approach to the atoning work of Christ, which concentrated upon his sufferings and death almost to the exclusion of the resurrection.

But even if Christ had not said these words—merely the fact that He, who is "the resurrection and the life," comes to the grave, is not this a sufficient sign that *this* sickness is not unto death, does not the fact that Christ *exists* mean that *this* sickness is not unto death?[30]

The words "Christ exists" are crucial, as we shall note in detail later. Presumably Kierkegaard found it unnecessary to deal with the resurrection as a basis for the continuing existence of Christ.

The event of the ascension is of considerable importance in Kierkegaard's thought. This event is more determinative than that of the resurrection for his stress on the presence of the living Christ in all ages. His sermon, "Christ Is the Way," based on the Acts' account of the ascension, relates all the details of the event as recorded there. He adds pointedly, "The ascension and the fact that Christ is the way shall certainly be discussed here."[31] He is not unaware of the doubts and problems men have had regarding this event (presumably reflecting both rationalism and biblical scholarship in his day):

The ascension breaks with or figures against all natural laws. . . . Perhaps even you, when you once think about it, doubt and say: "An ascension? It goes against all the laws of nature, against the spirit in nature."[32]

But in typically Kierkegaardian fashion he confronts the doubt:

How could you possibly think of announcing that you have a doubt when the answer must be: "Go out first and become an imitator in the strictest sense of the word. Only such a one has the right to talk." . . . Of them not one has doubted![33]

But when it is for a good cause—for otherwise it does not help, and then the relationship is one of battling against all merely human concepts: suffering because one does good, because one is right, because one is loving—when it is for a good cause you live forsaken, persecuted, mocked, impoverished, you will see that you will not doubt His ascension, for you will need it.[34]

Obviously Kierkegaard needed the ascension. This does not make it true, so that the need is father of the deed; rather, this made it true *for him.**

Kierkegaard's understanding of the living Christ after the ascension reflects more of this dialectical approach. Christ in glory is not the living Christ who speaks the words of invitation, "Come hither." "No, *He* maintains silence, it is the *lowly one* who speaks."[35] Jesus Christ stands there in his humiliation, "an everlasting picture"[36]—as in Thorvaldsen's statue in the cathedral in Copenhagen showing Christ with the outstretched arms. He gives the invitation to follow him in his humiliation and suffering and not be offended.

O Lord Jesus Christ, would that we also might be contemporary with Thee, see Thee in Thy true form and in the actual environment in which Thou didst walk here on earth; not in the form in which an empty and meaningless tradition, or a thoughtless and superstitious, or a gossipy historical tradition, has deformed Thee; for it is not in the form of abasement the believer sees Thee, and it cannot possibly be in the form of glory, in which no man has yet seen Thee. Would that we might see Thee as Thou art and wast and wilt be until Thy return in glory, see Thee as the sign of offense and the object of faith, the lowly man, and yet the Savior and Redeemer of the race, who out of love did come to earth in order to seek the lost, in order to suffer and to die, and yet sorely troubled as Thou wast, alas, at every step Thou didst take upon earth, every time Thou didst stretch out Thy hand to perform signs and wonders, and every time, without moving a hand, Thou didst suffer defencelessly the opposition of men—again and again Thou wast constrained to repeat: Blessed is he whosoever is not offended in Me. Would that we might see Thee thus, and then that for all this we might not be offended in Thee.[37]

All of this illustrates a fundamentally conservative interpretation of the Gospels, blended with Kierkegaard's existential concern. But despite his essential agreement with Lutheran orthodoxy regarding biblical criticism and theology, Kierkegaard would not be associated with "the establish-

---

*Cf.: "the thing is to find a truth which is true *for me*, to find *the idea for which I can live and die*" (*Journals*, p. 15).

ment." His dispute with orthodoxy was not in the realm of
critical studies of the Bible, but on the grounds of the
hermeneutics of the church as demonstrated above all in
preaching. It neither ignored nor denied the historical Jesus
—it lacked that courage!—but it romanticized him and tran-
quilized the offense of the Gospel. The "twaddle, twattle,
patter, smallness, mediocrity, playing at Christianity" which
is orthodoxy, where "for one certified hypocrite there are
100,000 twaddlers, for one certified heretic, 100,000 nincom-
poops, . . . [this] resembles true Christianity [only] in so
far as it is not heterodoxy or heresy."[38] It "makes a career
and a success in this world by depicting on Sundays"[39] how
Christ suffered and how truth must suffer in this world. In
fact, it accentuates Christ's sufferings in its preaching,[40] but
refuses to suffer with him. The consequence is a "sentimental
and effeminate paganism" which turns Christianity into
mythology and Christ into a mythological figure. At such an
accusation the orthodox preacher

becomes furious and blazes out: "Yes, but Christ is indeed the true
God, and therefore He is no mythological figure . . . one can see that
in his mild countenance." But if one can see that in Him, then he is
eo ipso a mythological figure.[41]

Such is the orthodox confusion of Christianity with child-
ishness. "Due to a light-minded and heavy-hearted dread
of making decisions," by Baptism and Christian education it
"puts off and puts off and so gets the thing of becoming a
Christian shoved so far back that it is decided before one
knows anything about it."[42]

But the new biblical criticism is cut from the same cloth
as orthodoxy, according to Kierkegaard. He has no objection
to certain aspects of criticism, especially philological scholarship. The problem is that such scholarship suffers from a
certain ambiguity: It constantly seems to be in labor pangs,
about to yield a result for faith, but nothing comes forth.[43]

The hostile critic rushes in, attacks the Bible; the "learned rescue corps rushes in to defend—and so it goes on indefinitely."[44] Or possibly a new document is discovered. Instead of clarifying the Scriptures, this only adds one more interpretation to seven existing ones; so there is more vacillation in action while the people await the consensus of the scholarly commentators.[45]

People treat the Scriptures so scientifically that they might quite as well be anonymous writings. Behold, from the moment the parenthetical [psychology, scientific exegesis, and philosophical theology] got going there naturally was plenty to do for *private-docents* and licentiates and paragraph-swallowers and squinters; afterwards, as more and more work was done in this direction, things went more and more backward for the category of being called by a revelation; it became an insignificance, a matter of indifference, with which finally every man could compete; and then it went so entirely out of fashion that in the last resort it became a great rarity to see anybody in the "equipage" [of receiving a revelation].[46]

No wonder that when Magister Adler proclaimed that he had had a direct revelation from Christ the church was confounded!

But it is not human . . . to cunningly produce interpretation and science and more science, one layer after another (in about the same way as a boy puts one or more napkins in his trousers when he is to get a thrashing)—it is not human that I put all this between the Word and myself and then give this interpretation and learning the name of earnestness and zeal for truth and let this busyness swell up into such prolixity that I never come to receive the impression of God's Word, never come to observe myself in the mirror.[47]

Orthodoxy and biblical criticism had both succumbed to the temptation of Christendom—lukewarmness. Ignored was the Absolute Paradox—a man who claimed to be God was born at a particular time in history, lived, suffered, and died, and confronts us with the either/or decision: faith or rejection. "Blessed is he who is not offended in me."

II. Existential Relationship of Contemporaneity to the Historical Jesus

We have noted how Kierkegaard assumed the traditional understanding of the historical Jesus, in the first sense of the phrase, in contrast to the growing interest in the historical Jesus, in the second sense. In his antagonism to orthodoxy's sentimentalizing of the life of Jesus, however, and as a consequence of his own continuing struggle "to become a Christian," he moved in the direction of what we have suggested as a third understanding of the historical Jesus—an existential relationship of contemporaneity. While throughout his life he continued to reaffirm the reliability of the traditional picture of Jesus, he developed this new direction in considerable detail in his later writings. At first this constituted a "project of thought,"[48] but subsequently it became the main thrust of his attack upon the established church.

Several factors contributed to this development. We have already suggested the determinative one, Kierkegaard's own life. There is no need to reconstruct here the details of his struggle, as recorded in the *Journals*, "to find a truth which is true *for me*"[49]: his melancholic relationship to his father, his engagement to Regine, the attack by the *Corsair*, and the affair of Pastor Adler. Underlying all these external realities was his encounter with ultimate reality in three transforming experiences: 1835, "the great earthquake, . . . guilt"[50]; 1838,

27

"an indescribable joy, . . . God makes saints out of sinners"[51];
and 1848, "the metamorphosis, . . . that sin is forgotten by
God."[52] In vivid contrast to this struggle for certainty were
the smooth evolution of the Christian life, as characterized
by the life and teachings of the Church of Denmark, and the
inevitable progress of reason and history depicted in the
philosophical system of Hegel.

The Church of Denmark we have noted above: "childish
Christianity,"[53] "moonlight and charity-school sentimentali-
ty,"[54] "deification of the established order,"[55] "impudent
Christendom,"[56] "a society of non-Christians"[57] in which
"the sign of offense and the object of faith" are made into a
kind of "divine Uncle George"[58] and "a good sort of chap
after all."[59]

"The System" was Kierkegaard's simple, sardonic way of
alluding to the philosophy of Hegel, which had found its
exponent in Bishop Martensen, who sought to "go beyond"[60]
Hegel, just as "the Master" (Hegel) had sought to "go
further"[61] than Christianity. Four points of Hegel's system
are relevant to our interest in Kierkegaard's existential approach to the historical Jesus. First, the ontological identity
of thought (reason) and being is extended to encompass the
whole of reality. For Hegel, pure thought (higher reason)
overcomes the dichotomy of subject and object, and medi-
ates all discontinuities: infinite/finite, God/man, eternity/
time, nature/history, faith/reason, theology/philosophy. Second, reason participates in a necessary dialectical self-move-
ment consisting of thesis, antithesis, and synthesis. Philo-
sophically speaking, essence necessarily appears, transforming itself into existence. Existence, therefore, is the being of
essence, or essential being—essence is existence.[62] In logical
categories, the idea goes out from itself and returns to itself,
encompassing and transforming its contradictions. To speak
theologically, God goes forth from himself as the Other and
returns to himself as Spirit, so arriving at self-consciousness.

In history—the "history of the spirit"—"the cunning of reason" leads Oriental and classical civilizations by a path of inevitable necessity toward the goal of the Western state. Third, truth is objective, universal, self-authenticating; reason is therefore able to settle all questions with certainty. Fourth, the real is the rational; the thinking self and the objects of thought are equivalent. Truth, therefore, is immediate, within thinking man.

An indirect stimulus for Kierkegaard's investigation may have been the further development of radical biblical studies. The first attempt at a historical reconstruction of the life of Jesus, that of Reimarus, was published by Lessing in 1778. In the subsequent half-century a half-dozen rationalistic lives appeared, including that by Paulus. Strauss's *Life of Jesus*—conceived along Hegelian lines of the unity of God and man in the God-manhood of Jesus—appeared in 1835-36, and was reissued in an unaltered fourth edition in 1840. Strauss's *Dogmatics* was published the same year. Both were promptly translated into Danish. In response to these translations, the theological faculty of the University of Copenhagen offered a prize:

> In as much as the authority of the New Testament books has been the object of repeated attacks in recent times, so that the faith and the church appear to be endangered, a philosophical inquiry is requested into the question, if and how far the Christian religion is conditional upon the authority of the books of the New Testament and upon their historical reliability.[63]

Indirectly, this may have been the immediate stimulus for Kierkegaard's attention to the problem.

His first response was *Philosophical Fragments* (1844), a parody on similar philosophical treatises, beginning with "A Project of Thought."[64] The problem of the paper is stated in abstract terms:

> Is an historical point of departure possible for an eternal consciousness; how can such a point of departure have any other than a

merely historical interest; is it possible to base an eternal happiness upon historical knowledge?[65]

Johannes Climacus, who is not a Christian, is the pseudonymous author. Appropriately the motto is, "Better well hung than ill wed,"[66] i.e., better to be hung in paradox with the Crucified One than to be wed to a worldly philosophical system.[67] The following year *Concluding Unscientific Postscript to the Philosophical Fragments* was completed. In this extensive attack upon "the System," "the historical costume"[68] of the *Fragments* is made explicit. Again Johannes Climacus is the author. The Introduction, "How may I, Johannes Climacus, participate in the happiness promised by Christianity?"[69] confirms the subtitle, "An Existential Contribution." Seven years later (after the metamorphosis of 1848) *The Sickness unto Death* and *Training in Christianity* moved vigorously from the medium of indirect communication to direct Christian proclamation under the ironic pseudonym Anti-Climacus, "a Christian in an extraordinary degree,"[70] who drives the existential categories to an extraordinary degree.

The basis of Kierkegaard's existential interpretation of the historical Jesus in these writings is his epistemological quarrel with Hegel. We have extracted four relevant points from the system upon the basis of Kierkegaard's dialectic in these volumes. With respect to the first point, Kierkegaard asserts a "metaphysical crochet."[71] It is the paradoxical nature of the passion of reason to seek a collision with something which it cannot think. But this passion is the downfall of reason. It collides with the Unknown. If the Unknown does not exist, it would be impossible to prove it (and foolish to try); if it does not exist, it cannot be proved by reason or it would no longer be the Unknown. The Unknown is the limit to which reason repeatedly comes—something absolutely different which it cannot even conceive. The existence of the

Unknown is therefore elusive as far as reason is concerned. The theological expression for this is Kierkegaard's fundamental presupposition, the infinite qualitative difference between God and man.

Secondly, Kierkegaard questions the basic dialectical movement of Hegel's system: that essence necessarily appears as existence. A logical system may be possible, but its claim that it begins with nothing is ridiculous.[72] Prior to any movement of the idea is the thinker himself, who cannot objectively forget that he exists. "I always reason from existence, not towards existence."[73] "All understanding comes after the fact."[74] One does not prove that a stone exists, but that something existing is a stone. One does not prove Napoleon's existence from his deeds, since there is no absolute relationship between Napoleon and his deeds—someone else may have done them. God's deeds do exist in an absolute relationship to him. But if I am to prove God's existence by his deeds, how am I to know which deeds are his and which are not? If I seek to establish which deeds can prove his existence, I presuppose his existence by the attempt. His existence thus emerges from the demonstration only by a leap. A gap exists between the idea in my mind and his existence. Only as I "let the proof go"[75] do I see that existence. Whoever attempts to prove God's existence, therefore, proves something that does not need proof and which, if it is sought, can only confirm the presupposition that God does—or does not—exist.

In similar fashion, the dialectical movement of the idea is confronted with Kierkegaard's stress on the reality of the thinking subject in time and space. The negative of the idea as it goes forth from itself presupposes the experience of the thinker and an intuition of time and space.[76] According to "the System," pure thought envelops time and space, infinite and finite. To Kierkegaard, finite and infinite are mutually contradictory; they repel each other.[77]

Most relevant to our purposes is the "Interlude" in the *Fragments*.[78] Here the historical aspect of the dialectical movement is discussed. Change presupposes the existence of that which changes. But that which has come into being—becoming—is different from that which it was before it came into being. Thus nonbeing is possibility; what it has become is actuality. A transition takes place from possibility to actuality, involving a kind of suffering. The necessary, on the other hand, cannot undergo any change, cannot suffer the transition from possibility to actuality. It *is* because it is necessary; it cannot come into being. The necessary, therefore, is also eternal; in its perfection it can have no history. But what comes into being cannot be necessary. Neither the possible nor the actual is necessary. No becoming is necessary—it has taken place in freedom. What may appear to be intervening causes have themselves come into being, and all refer ultimately back to a free cause. History, therefore, is that which has come into being; it is the realm of becoming, where possibility has become actuality. What has happened has happened as it happened; it cannot be changed. This is the inevitability of the past. But this does not mean that it had to happen of necessity, in the way it did. It did not become necessary by coming into being; rather by coming into being it proved that it was not necessary. It was free; but it is no longer free to change, since it is past. So also with the future. It cannot be predicted, since possibility is free to come into actuality in the same way as it has in the past.

A subject's apprehension of the past cannot change it, even though the distance of time produces an illusion of necessity. Knowledge of the past confers no necessity upon it—it could have happened differently. A "prophet of the past" expresses this fact—that the actuality of the past is based on no necessity, that possibility has become actuality in freedom. Hence the historian's sense of wonder as he confronts the mystery of the past and the element of uncertainty in that which came to be.

How is the knowledge of the past apprehended? No immediate sensation and cognition (which, in the scientific sense, are certain, according to Kierkegaard) can be had of becoming, since there is an elusiveness implicit in all becoming. The sensory perception of an event is not of its historicity, but only the impression of the presence of some content about which the senses do not deceive. In order to apprehend the past an organ analogous with the historical itself is necessary—one which can grasp the uncertainty of all becoming as it is involved in the free transition from possibility to actuality. Faith ("direct faith," "belief")* has this function, for in the certainty of belief there is always a negative uncertainty corresponding to the uncertainty of becoming. Thus sensory knowledge may affirm the *what* of a happening—the natural phenomena associated with the historical event—since no uncertainty is involved at this point. But the *that* of a happening—the historical event, which is related to the transition from possibility to actuality without necessity—can be affirmed only by faith. The uncertainty of becoming can be resolved only by an act of the will. Faith *believes* the past, overcoming the uncertainty within itself. It believes the *that* without knowing the *how* or denying the possibility of another *that*. Faith, therefore, always runs the risk of committing an error; but it still believes. "There is no other road to faith; if one wishes to escape risk, it is as if one wanted to know with certainty that he can swim before going into the water."[79] But faith is not another kind of knowledge alongside of sensory knowledge. It is a sense

---

*It is to be noted that the reference to faith here and throughout this paragraph is not to faith in the Christian sense of the word. The distinction between faith as an act of the will giving historical contemporaneity ("direct faith") and faith as both a leap and a response giving believing contemporaneity ("eminent faith") will be clarified below.

for becoming. It is the opposite of doubt, which protests against the conclusions of faith arrived at without immediate assurance. Only by an act of the will does faith exclude doubt. In the situation of a noncontemporary with an event, the testimony of contemporaries takes the place of immediate sensation and cognition—it can demonstrate to him the *what* of some fact of becoming. The distance from the event makes no difference, since the uncertain quality which is implicit in all becoming is always present after the event. A successor knows, to be sure, on account of the testimony of some contemporary; but only by taking the testimony up into his consciousness and giving it his assent, thus making it historical for himself, can he believe the *that* of the event. No contemporary can believe by virtue of (sensory) immediacy alone; neither can any successor believe solely by virtue of the testimony he has before him. The only contemporaneity with a historical event, therefore, is that of direct faith.

We have already come to the third point in Hegel's system, the objectivity of truth.[80] Objective truth is possible in the realm of the physical sciences, but not elsewhere. The theory of objective, universal truth involves two corresponding errors. It makes of life a parenthesis and it forgets that the thinker is an existing individual. It makes the individual something accidental and his existence something impersonal, universal, and eternal. It tries to think of existence apart from the passionate personal experience of the exister. *To be* means to be an existing individual; to be an existing individual means to be involved in the moment of decision—to be a subjective thinker. "Truth is subjectivity!"[81] With respect to God, he is Subject, not object. Man's relationship to him, therefore, must be in passionate inwardness, in personal knowing, not in any objective approximation process.

Fourth, Kierkegaard poses "a project of thought" for poet

and philosopher: What if the Socratic presupposition that truth is recollected by the teacher's maieutic assistance were not true? Suppose the learner were in error.[82] Then the teacher would be unable to help him recollect the truth. He must both grant him the condition necessary for understanding the truth and give him the truth itself. Since error is polemic to truth, the teacher must transform the learner. He must beget the truth in him. This only "the God"[83] can do. Hence the teacher must be both Savior and Teacher. In the moment, the fullness of time, he must create the condition and bestow the truth; he must save and teach. But how can one in sin—for such is error—know the God, who is totally unlike him in his (the God's) perfection? And how can the God make the unequal equal, without destroying the freedom of the learner to respond of his own will? "Suppose there was a king who loved a humble maiden. . . ."[84] Neither in the elevation of the maiden nor in the majestic appearance of the king could love be made happy. The king will appear in the form of a servant, and so love will find equality with the beloved. The God becomes man, in servant form—no mere outer garment, but a true incognito. He runs the risk of misunderstanding and offense, experiencing all things with the lowest, including death. So the God desires in love to be equal with the lowest and the humblest.

This is the Miracle, the Absolute Paradox. The Unknown is known; God becomes man, a man; the infinite becomes finite; that which of necessity is enters into becoming; the impossible becomes actuality; unlikeness is found in likeness. The consequence: offense—or faith.

*   *   *

Having dealt with the philosophical methodology which Kierkegaard uses against Hegel, we must now finally turn to its specific reference to the historical Jesus and faith's relation to him. To do this we shall separate the discussion by means of the double dialectic which Kierkegaard depicts in several ways:

A. THE HISTORICAL FACT	B. THE ABSOLUTE FACT
the objective problem	the subjective problem
What happened?	How do I become a Christian?
what and/or that	how
Jesus of Nazareth	the Absolute Paradox
uncertain	absurd
historical contemporaneity	believing contemporaneity
direct faith—man's will	eminent faith—God grants the condition
approximation	appropriation
the learner	the disciple

These two "facts" cannot be separated; but for the sake of understanding Kierkegaard's existential approach to the historical Jesus, this more or less arbitrary division should prove helpful. "An existential system is impossible!"[85]

A. The Historical Fact—the Objective Problem

What can we know about the life of Jesus of Nazareth? Is it possible to be certain of the biographical details of his life? Can we know for sure that he really lived? Is there any certainty regarding him? In one sense of the word such questions appear to pose an objective problem. There are historical events to be dealt with, and the questions may be asked without any reference to the relationship of the historical facts to one's "eternal blessedness." We have noted in some detail Kierkegaard's disagreement with Hegel, particularly in the "Interlude" discussion of the two ways in which the historical may be apprehended: by immediate sensation and cognition of the natural phenomena of the event, and by the resolve of direct faith in the becoming of the event. How, then, does Kierkegaard handle the historical fact of Jesus of Nazareth?

First, there were immediately contemporary eyewitnesses to his life. Two types (a third will be introduced later) are suggested by Kierkegaard.[86] One followed him more closely than the pilot-fish the shark—armed, as it were, today with a motion picture camera—to record every event and detail for posterity. For such a contemporary Jesus was the occasion for an abundance of historical knowledge. The *what* of what happened he could report with precision. If someone disputed with him about the accuracy of his report, he could point to what he had seen—or simply wash his hands of the accusation. He knew what he had seen. But his conclusions would not necessarily be related to what he had seen. He might say that he saw nothing extraordinary about the man. Or he might be inclined to praise Jesus for what he had done, enthusiastically trumpeting his gratitude for all the things he had seen. When Jesus died, he could have painted a portrait or a series of descriptive scenes. But none of this would have made him a disciple. He was simply an eyewitness.

Another followed Jesus—with tape-recorder, today—intent upon transcribing every word that was said, for in the teachings of Jesus he had found a new self-understanding. Compared with this new understanding of himself in the light of eternity, any knowledge of Jesus himself was accidental and simply historical; ultimately it was merely a matter of memory. And even that memory could pass away without sorrow—this Socrates hoped would happen to the memory of him, once he had maieutically brought forth the recollection of eternal truth from his pupils. For such a contemporary, the historical event was simply an occasion; the teacher, a midwife. The eternal alone was important. Such a one, therefore, intent upon the newly-acquired self-understanding which he had received, was not a disciple of Jesus.

Each of these eyewitnesses had certain advantages over

later generations. He had the benefit of immediate sensation and cognition, and such immediacy is not subject to error (according to Kierkegaard).[87] He could have a high degree of certainty about the *what* of the life of Jesus, i.e., the details of his life and his teachings. This could be thought to be an advantage. In addition, he was free from the chatter and rumor which, in the "echo of the centuries"[88] of ecclesiastical life, have blurred and confused the purity of the report of the things which were first seen and heard. "But let him look to his conclusions."[89] In spite of immediate certainty regarding physical details, such an eyewitness could not know by immediate cognition *that* this event had come into being. He had immediate contemporaneity with Jesus of Nazareth —something no other generation can have. But historical contemporaneity with the historical fact *that* Jesus had existed—this involves not just sensory impression, but the act of the will affirming the "thatness" of Jesus. It involves faith. He could never simply believe his eyes. He could never have proved that Jesus existed, for no necessity is involved in historical becoming. Apart from (direct) faith, he could never be sure that Jesus really existed. That he could affirm by a passionate resolve, overcoming the uncertainty by faith.[90]

A corresponding disadvantage of the immediately contemporary eyewitness was that in his absorption with the facts as he experienced them he may well have missed "the splendor" not apparent to the senses.[91] Such a contemporary would hardly be called happy! Additionally, there was for the immediately contemporary person the scandal that here a man, a mere human individual, had come into collision with the established order.[92] This, plus his obscure origin, the company he kept, the extravagant claims he made for himself, his signs and wonders, and above all his death—all of these made the possibility of offense tremendous.[93] At least the offense could have served to rouse attention, to induce a state of mind demanding a deeper decision with respect to Jesus—whether to follow or reject him.[94] But this was a fearful advantage! How problematical, therefore, it was to be immediately contemporary, to be even a learner; even more, how problematical it was to be a disciple.

Secondly, what about the non-immediately contemporary person, one of a later generation—the "disciple at second hand"?[95] Perhaps the first generation after the immediate eyewitnesses had some advantage (for example, the evangelists). A man in such a time could have had access to some of the witnesses still living and their associates. From them, surely, he could have obtained a most reliable account, overcoming discrepancies, supplementing reports, and thus knowing more than any single eyewitness could have known. But only historically speaking was this an advantage. In a deeper sense there would have been another doubtful advantage, that of being closer (than later generations) to the shock of offense produced by Jesus. Only this shock could have made the first-generation learner anything more than a second-hand observer or spectator.

In later generations the situation is essentially the same. No longer can anyone become immediately contemporary with Jesus of Nazareth. The preacher may romantically yearn—in his sermon—to be such,[96] and the congregation may sentimentally wish to be with Jesus in the garden (and literary and cinematic efforts may attempt to transcend the centuries so that "you are there" "the day Jesus died"). They can hardly be stopped, says Kierkegaard; but in spite of their highly organized fellowship and pilgrimages, they "will none the less scarcely discover the holy land (in an immediate sense), since it is not to be found either on the map or on the earth."[97]

All generations are dependent upon reports of eyewitnesses for the historical facts of Jesus' life. "The Scriptures present themselves as documents of decisive significance."[98]

They serve the same function for later generations that immediate sensation and cognition served for eyewitnesses. Historical and critical scholarship—what Kierkegaard calls "objective scholarship"—seeks diligently to establish some certainty regarding these records: "the canonicity of the individual books, their authenticity, their integrity, the trustworthiness of their authors."[99] But the nature of a historical document like the New Testament is that it can readily beguile the inquirer[100] into treating it so objectively that he slips into a parenthesis that may last a whole lifetime—or even centuries in the church. His conclusions as to what the Scriptures say happened in Jesus' life—or what he thinks really happened—may be arrived at without any concern for the actuality of Jesus' existence. Did he really live? That can be affirmed only when the "parenthesis-hound" ceases to be a spectator and passionately affirms in the face of all skeptical doubt *that* Jesus existed. But this leap of (direct) faith still does not make a disciple of a person of the later generation any more than of one immediately contemporary with Jesus.

Does the "last generation" have any advantage in the "naturalization"[101] of the fact throughout many centuries, i.e., that being a Christian has become almost second nature to humanity? "Many good and upright people up here on the hill have believed, i.e., have said that they have believed."[102] This greater ease in being a Christian in Christendom is at most a dubious advantage. More likely it is a danger precisely the opposite of that of the first generation. The shock of offense has been so absorbed by Christendom that no decision of faith seems necessary.

Dear husband of mine. . . . How can you doubt that you are a Christian? Are you not a Dane, and does not the geography say that the Lutheran form of the Christian religion is the ruling religion in Denmark? For you are surely not a Jew, nor are you a Mohammedan; what then can you be if you are not a Christian? It is a thousand years since paganism was driven out of Denmark, so I know you are not a pagan. Do you not perform your duties at the office like a conscientious civil servant; are you not a good citizen of a Christian nation, a Lutheran Christian state? So then of course you must be a Christian.[103]

What is the conclusion to the objective problem of the historical fact of Jesus of Nazareth? It is impossible to return to the year 30 A.D. and become immediately contemporaneous with Jesus. In the New Testament, however, we have the record of eyewitnesses to their encounter with him. This is the source of our knowledge of what happened in his life, and biblical scholarship continues to seek clarity regarding this knowledge. But "when Christianity is viewed from the standpoint of its historical documentation . . . nothing is more readily evident than that the greatest attainable certainty . . . is merely an *approximation*."[104] It is a relationship of the mind to certain historical facts. *That* Jesus existed, however, is a decision which the will, the whole self, must make by (direct) faith. Only then does one become historically contemporaneous with the existence of Jesus of Nazareth. Faith is an objective uncertainty held fast in the passion of inwardness.

But even the resolve which produces historical contemporaneity does not make one a disciple! It deals only with the dialectic of our relationship to the objective problem of Jesus of Nazareth. It gives an answer to the important question: Did Jesus exist? But it has not yet encountered the second dialectic: the Absolute Paradox, that this man claimed to be God, and the subjective problem: How do I become a Christian? In words that carry this concern to the extreme, Kierkegaard says:

Can one learn from history anything about Christ? No. Why not? Because one can "know" nothing at all about "Christ"; He is the paradox, the object of faith, existing only for faith. But all historical communication is communication of "knowledge," hence from history one can learn nothing about Christ. For if one learns little or much about Him, or anything at all, He (who is thus known) is not He who in truth He is, i.e., one learns to know nothing about Him, or one learns to know something incorrect about Him, one is deceived. History makes out Christ to be another than He truly is, and so one learns to know a lot about . . . Christ? No, not about Christ, for about Him nothing can be known, He can only be believed.[105]

B. The Absolute Fact—the Subjective Problem

Fundamental to this second level of the discussion is Kierkegaard's basic presupposition (contravening Hegel's system and Strauss's Hegelian *Life of Jesus*), the infinite qualitative difference between God and man.

> God and man are two qualities between which there is an infinite qualitative difference. Every doctrine which overlooks this difference is, humanly speaking, crazy; understood in a godly sense, it is blasphemy. In paganism [and Hegelianism] man made God a man (the man-God); in Christianity God makes Himself man (the God-Man).[106]

The misfortune of Christendom is that by absorbing the Hegelian principle of the unity of all reality this distinction is pantheistically abolished,[107] and the tension of the paradox is relaxed.[108] Man has the "optical illusion"[109] that the God-Man personifies the realization of the essential unity of God and humanity. What is ignored (in terms of our survey of Kierkegaard's opposition to Hegel)? Sin, the individual, above all, the Absolute Paradox and the subjective problem of faith.

Returning, then, to our question of the historical Jesus, reason is brought up short by a second thrust of the dialectic. This historical fact, which sensory perception can describe and direct faith must affirm to have existed—this historical fact has a peculiar character which distinguishes it from every other historical fact.

> The dialectical contradiction [is] that the historical fact here in question is not a simple historical fact, but is constituted by that which only against its nature can become historical, hence by virtue of the absurd.[110]

"He said—ah, it was *He* that said it—that He was God!"[111]
This fact is based on a self-contradiction. The eternal entered time, God became man, that which by its nature cannot become historical became historical in the historical
individual, Jesus of Nazareth. The old philosophical question "Does God exist?" is confronted by a new assertion. It
is not merely that God does exist, but he exists as a man.
The limits of reason have not only been reached, they have
been surpassed. To reason, the Absolute Paradox is absurd.
This is not because the offended reason has discovered the
Paradox and then holds aloof from it *quia absurdum.* This
is the "acoustic illusion."[112] Reason thinks it hears a paradox
it has discovered. Rather, the Absolute Paradox, the moment
it comes into being, makes reason absurd, declares "reason
a blockhead and a dunce, capable at the most of saying yes
and no to the same thing."[113] Man, the connoisseur of self-
knowledge, who thinks that truth and God are within himself, in his immanent religiousness (religion A), is be-
wildered. He had thought that his nature partook of the
divine, and so he could know God. But the Absolute Paradox
renders the paradox still more appalling. "The same paradox
has the double aspect which proclaims it as the Absolute
Paradox; negatively by revealing the absolute unlikeness of
sin, positively by proposing to do away with the absolute
unlikeness in absolute likeness."[114] In such a case, the Teacher
cannot be dismissed with no claim upon the pupil, *à la*
Socrates, once the eternal fact had been conceived. The
Teacher, unmoved by anything but love,[115] makes himself
known as Teacher and Savior. This is the absolute fact—not
just a historical fact or an eternal fact.

"The subjective problem: the relation of the subject to the
truth of Christianity—the problem of becoming a Christian."[116] How can I base my eternal happiness upon such a
fact? How can I be contemporaneous with this Teacher?

Kierkegaard again uses, in this context, the situation of the

immediately contemporary eyewitness and the non-immediately contemporary person. There was a third eyewitness
who had nothing of the extended contact with Jesus as had
the other two. Possibly he was out of the country and re-
turned only for the last days of Holy Week. Even then he
had other important engagements in connection with the
Passover, and was brought into contact with Jesus only at
the last minutes of his servant-life (Simon of Cyrene, for
example). But this historical ignorance could not prevent
him from becoming a disciple any more than the abundance
of historical knowledge could make the other two eyewitnesses into disciples.[117] In fact, later he would discover that
his very ignorance had a certain advantage to it. The other
eyewitnesses, and potentially he, were so tempted to devote
themselves to seeing and hearing physically that the whole
procedure turned out to be a waste of effort, even a dan-
gerous toil.[118] They missed what was crucial for faith. In fact,
it was possible that this third contemporary could have met
Jesus on the street some time later, or walked some distance
with him on the way (to Emmaus!) without realizing who
he was. But this would not have proved that he had ceased
to be a disciple.[119] This is not to say, however, that the out-
ward figure of Jesus was a matter of indifference to him. God
opened for him the eyes of faith so that he could see what
the other eyewitnesses could not see with their human eyes
of sight. For him, "the Moment became decisive for eternity."[120] This was no mere historical fact, as it was for the first
eyewitness; no mere eternal fact, as for the second. This was
for him the absolute fact, the eternal moment, "the fulness
of time."[121]

How did the eyewitness become a disciple? In the moment
of encounter he became aware of his error (which was not
merely the absence of truth but polemic to the truth), and
rejected the offense. In the moment he was given the condition by which he might understand truth. In the moment

he was given truth. Christianly speaking, he became conscious of sin, was converted from sin to grace, repented his former state, was born again, was thus made a new creature. Christ was the begetter of truth in him; he was Savior, Redeemer, Atoner, and Judge. The historical fact had served

as an occasion by means of which the contemporary . . . receives the condition from the God, and so beholds his glory with the eyes of faith. Aye, happy such a contemporary! But such a contemporary is not in the immediate sense an eyewitness; he is contemporary as a believer, in the autopsy of Faith [i.e., faith's own way of seeing things].[122]

What of the non-immediate contemporary, a man of a later generation, such as Johannes Climacus? For such a one the reports of eyewitness disciples are indispensable. In addition, predecessors in the church who witness to their faith can inform him that they have believed the fact and in this form of communication relate to him something of the content of the fact. This communication ought to be given in such a manner that the ambiguity and offense which aroused the attention of eyewitnesses might do the same for the potential disciple of a later generation. Especially after many centuries of the naturalization of Christianity a repellant is needed, making it difficult again to become a Christian. "Since the circumstances are so radically changed, the clergy should . . . win men by deterring them."[123]

But the credibility of the testimony to Jesus Christ or the accuracy of the details is not determinative for faith. Faith is related to the historical fact, but not to a simple historical fact that demands explicit accuracy.

Here this is not the case, for Faith cannot be distilled from even the nicest accuracy of detail. The historical fact that the God has been in human form is the essence of the matter; the rest of the historical detail is not even as important as if we had to do with a human being instead of with the God. Jurists say that a capital crime submerges all lesser crimes, and so it is with Faith. Its absurdity makes all petty difficulties vanish. Inconsistencies which would otherwise be disconcerting do not count for anything here; they make no difference whatsoever. . . . If the contemporary generation had left nothing behind them but these words: "We have believed that in such and such a year the God appeared among us in the humble figure of a servant, that he lived and taught in our community, and finally died," it would be more than enough. The contemporary generation would have done all that was necessary; for this little advertisement, this *nota bene* on a page of universal history, would be sufficient to afford an occasion for a successor, and the most voluminous account can in all eternity do nothing more.[124]

Faith itself cannot be communicated so that another believes because of the testimony of believers. Such reports are only the occasion by which the living Christ confronts the learner. He "believes *by means of* (this expresses the occasional) the testimony . . . and *in virtue of* the condition he himself receives from the God."[125] Thus the reports of eyewitnesses and predecessors perform the same function for him that immediate contemporaneity (immediate sensation and cognition) did for the eyewitness. The situation is identical, therefore, for later generations as for the immediate contemporaries of Jesus. All generations are essentially alike in this: it is "equally difficult but also equally easy" to become a Christian, "since the God grants the condition."[126]

Any testimony that is different from this which we have described does not serve as an occasion for faith, and may well be harmful to the possibility for faith. It is either history, as when a historian recounts one act among many others, or philosophy, which does not deal with the Object of faith.[127] If one proposes to believe because of others, he is a fool and might just as well believe a Münchhausen.[128]

Alas! one may be sure that this will create a tremendous sensation, and give occasion for the writing of folios; for this counterfeit earnestness, which asks whether so-and-so is trustworthy instead of whether the inquirer himself has faith, is an excellent mask for spiritual indolence, and for town gossip on a European scale.[129]

If such is the case, the witness himself has become the object of faith to the believer; the witness has become "the

God for a third party."[130] "God alone grants the condition."
It is in this context that Kierkegaard's sarcastic scorn of
those who seek the probabilities and proofs for faith must
be placed.

> The shrewd and prudent man feels his way with the understanding
> in the realm of the probable, and finds God where the probabilities
> are favorable, and gives thanks on the great holidays of probability,
> when he has acquired a good livelihood, . . . when he has got himself
> a pretty and attractive wife. . . .[131]

This objectively perverse appropriation-process is the
exact opposite of faith's subjective appropriation. It begins
with possibility, proceeds by ascending degrees of probability, and finally after long deliberation is ready to believe.

> And lo, now it has become precisely impossible to believe it. Any-
> thing that is . . . probable . . . is something he can . . . *know*—but
> it is impossible to *believe*. For the absurd is the object of faith, and
> the only object that can be believed.[132]

Particularly singled out for Kierkegaard's ridicule are the
"sweating orators,"[133] the "theocentric helpers,"[134] who with
their "affected religious eloquence"[135] imagine themselves to
be "prosecuting attorneys for Deity."[136] They rush to the
assistance of God, bringing their "erring *Wissenschaft*"[137]
so that they may secure an entirely trustworthy account of
the biblical faith in Jesus Christ. The moment they join the
scholars it is inevitable that the Scriptures be studied with
thorough historical and critical discipline. And what if these
conservative critics, in their comical "imported passion" that
is not faith but fanaticism,[138] should succeed in proving
about the Bible everything that in their happiest moments
they wished to prove? This brings faith no nearer. Rather,
their prodigious efforts will only confuse faith with knowledge, and so prove to be a danger, not a help. All the apologetic efforts of orthodox Christianity to make Christianity
plausible would, if successful, add up to the ironic triumph
of having entirely quashed Christianity.[139] Not only is the

existence of Jesus beyond the results of this approximation-process; his existence as the God-Man "for me" is two leaps beyond. If approximation is the only certainty attainable for historical knowledge, it is totally inadequate for one's eternal blessedness. So the beautiful dream of the conservative critics is shattered.

Or what if the antagonistic critics succeeded in proving even more than their most passionate hostility ever desired? Is Christianity abolished? Their conclusions prove nothing about the historical existence of Jesus, and the believer is still free to assert his faith in Christ. Faith, therefore, might preferably be content with the Scriptures as they are, "as a profitable schoolmaster in . . . uncertainty."[140] Then there is no temptation to eliminate the passion of faith in the face of the uncertain (the historical fact) and the absurd (the absolute fact). No wonder Kierkegaard felt "as welcome as a dog in a game of bowls"[141] among the biblical critics!

Any appeal to a "dogmatic guaranty"[142] for the authority of the Scriptures, e.g., the doctrine of inspiration, is equally untenable. Inspiration is an object of faith, so its relationship to criticism is ambiguous and its circular argument for biblical infallibility useless. The same is true regarding any security through an appeal to other authorities for faith in Christ—to the miracles,[143] to the pope,[144] to the Grundtvigian triad of the living word in the church, creed, and Sacraments,[145] to Baptism in particular,[146] to the ordination of the clergy,[147] or, even more, to the proof of history, i.e., the eighteen hundred years since Christ lived.[148] To each of these authorities (most of which Christians had recourse to in the face of growing doubts about the Bible) the same criticism applies as to the appeal to the Bible itself: the dialectic of faith is ignored. Worse, faith is idolatrously placed in these authorities.

But what does [all this] prove? At the most it might prove that Jesus Christ was a great man, perhaps the greatest of all; but that He was . . . God—nay, stop there! The conclusion shall by God's help never be drawn.[149]

For the sake of absolute clarity, however, we must reaffirm that Kierkegaard is not the champion of subjectivity (as he is often portrayed), who was blind to the objective givenness of Christianity. He is not suggesting the elimination of these forms of authority from the Christian faith. He is protesting against their perversion by which human authorities are used to subvert the authority—the self-attesting authority—of Christ, the Absolute Paradox, and so make faith synonymous with a pleasant inward religiosity. It is the very nature of the paradox-faith that it demands the proper recognition of "the most important ethical-religious concept —authority."[150] In the midst of the confusion of the church in its dealings with Magister Adler (who had claimed divine authority for a special revelation), Kierkegaard wrote extensively "on authority and revelation,"* pointing to the divine authority which distinguishes an apostle from a genius. "Christ as the God-Man is in possession of the specific quality of authority which no eternity can mediate and put Christ on the same plane with the essential human equali-

---

On Authority and Revelation is the title Walter Lowrie (as translator) gave to Kierkegaard's unpublished notes for what Kierkegaard first called "The Book on Adler." It is significant that a year before the revolutions of 1848 in Europe and prior to "the metamorphosis" (after which he knew that he "must speak" against the abuses of the church), Kierkegaard wrote "without authority" (xxvii) in the second Preface: "The misfortune of our age . . . is disobedience, unwillingness to obey. And one deceives oneself and others by wishing to make us imagine that it is doubt. No, it is insubordination: it is not doubt of religious truth but insubordination against religious authority which is the fault in our misfortune and the cause of it. But, dialectically, insubordination has two forms: either wishing to cast down the ruler or wishing to be the ruler—and so religiously: either wishing to be a Feuerbach or wishing wilfully to be an apostle. Disobedience is the secret of the religious confusion of our age" (xviii).

Kierkegaard's violent attack upon Christendom, particularly the church, at the end of his life must be seen in the context of these previous assertions. He stood in dialectical relation to the authority of the church, not rebelling against it, but, like Luther, attacking the church in the name of

ty."[151] The apostle's authority rests in that of Christ. The apostle, therefore,

should according to God's ordinance assert his divine authority to chase away all impertinent people who will not obey him but argue. And instead of obeying, men transform an apostle into an examinee who comes as it were to the marketplace with a new doctrine.[152]

So also "a sermon operates absolutely and certainly through authority, that of Holy Writ and Christ's apostles."[153]

But there is inherent in authority a dialectical quality. While possessing divine authority, the apostle can give no visible evidence to it. "It is nonsense to get *sensible* certitude that an apostle is an apostle (the paradoxical determinant of a spiritual connection), just as it is nonsense to get *sensible* certitude that God exists."[154] The authority is recognized only by the one who has already yielded to *the* authority in faith. All derivative Christian authorities, therefore, have a task corresponding to the dialectic in the role of John the Baptist: they are precursors to Christ (see "the occasion," above). Christ

draws the precursor within the sphere of his authority and by virtue of his authority confirms him as being the genuine precursor. The word of the precursor . . . is only to be believed after Christ has confirmed the fact that the precursor really is the precursor.[155]

Hence we have a situation identical to that discussed previously with respect to the function of the Scriptures in the faith of later generations.

*   *   *

---

the church's authority so that it might again properly exercise its authority.

Another aspect of his attitude toward authority is to be seen in his purpose for using the pseudonyms. "My purpose in life would seem to be to present the truth as I discover it in such a way as simultaneously to destroy all possible authority. By ceasing to have authority, by being in the greatest possible degree unreliable in the eyes of men, I present the truth and put them in a contradictory position from which they can only save themselves by making the truth their own" (*Journals*, p. 117).

In the second chapter of this book we have discussed what we have called the existential relationship of contemporaneity to the historical Jesus, as Kierkegaard perceives it. In effect it is a dialectical relationship of objective fact and subjective faith.

The Scriptures and the authorities of Christianity tell us of a man, Jesus of Nazareth. We can no longer be immediately contemporaneous with him, but we may be with these instrumentalities. Therefore they may be subjected to critical scrutiny to determine the validity of their evidence regarding what happened in the life of Jesus. But the question of the actual existence of Jesus cannot be settled by such objectivity, but only by the decision of faith affirming this truth in the face of the approximate knowledge we have of him. Hence by (direct) faith we can overcome the objective uncertainty and be historically contemporaneous with him.

But inseparable from this historical fact is its uniqueness, that Jesus said that he was God, that, in effect, in the form of the suffering servant is found the incarnation of God in his love. The absurdity of this fact is that it offends not only our intellect but the very nature of our understanding of ourselves as religious persons. Only by the leap of faith can we appropriate this truth in the face of the absurdity of the Paradox. Hence (eminent) faith overcomes the offense in the passion of inwardness, and we can be believing contemporaries with Jesus Christ.*

---

*It is not within the scope of this book to discuss further Kierkegaard's fundamental exposition of the second aspect of the absolute fact—the subjective problem, the "how." In all of his works, but particularly in the *Postscript* and *Training in Christianity*, appear the categories by which he describes various aspects of faith: the leap, decision; inwardness, subjectivity, passion; immediacy after reflection, contemporaneity with Christ, repetition, the movement of infinity; offense, suffering, crucifixion of the understanding, the martyrdom of believing; etc.

Also, it should be noted that the tension of faith that is apparent in both direct faith and eminent faith continues throughout life, for one is always—and only—in the process of "becoming a Christian."

But the additional uniqueness of this historical fact is that while "faith is an objective uncertainty held fast in an appropriation process of the most passionate inwardness,"[156] faith is also a gift of God through this historical person Jesus Christ. He it is who encounters us in the moment, makes us conscious of our sins, gives us the possibility for receiving the truth, and begets the truth within us. Hence it is the historical Jesus who is contemporary with us as the living Lord who "from on high . . . will draw all unto himself."[157]

Kierkegaard's own summary of "the dialectic of becoming a Christian" states:

Socrates did not first of all get together some proofs of the immortality of the soul in order then to live in that belief, on the strength of the proofs. The very reverse is the case; he said: the possibility of there being an immortality occupies me to such a degree that I unquestionably stake my whole life upon it as though it were the most certain of all things. And so he lived—and his life is a proof of the immortality of the soul. He did not believe merely on the strength of the proofs and then live; no, his life is the proof, and only with his martyr's death is the proof complete. . . .

Carefully used that may be adapted to the problem of becoming a Christian.

First of all there is, quite rightly, the doubt (Lessing's) whether one can base eternal happiness upon something historical.

And consequently there is something historical, the story of Jesus Christ.

But now is the historical fact quite certain? To this one must answer: even though it were the most certain of all historical facts it would be of no help, there cannot be any *direct* transition from an historical fact to the foundation upon it of an eternal happiness. That is something qualitatively new.

How then do we proceed? Thus. A man says to himself, à la Socrates: Here is an historical fact which teaches me that in regard to my eternal happiness I must have recourse to Jesus Christ. Now I must certainly preserve myself from taking the wrong turning into scientific enquiry and research, as to whether it is quite certainly historical; for it is historical right enough; and if it were ten times as certain in all its details it would still be no help: for *directly* I cannot be helped.

And so I say to myself: I choose; that historical fact means so much to me that I decide to stake my whole life upon that if. Then he lives; lives entirely full of the idea, risking his life for it; and his life is the proof that he believes. He did not have a few proofs, and so believed and then began to live. No, the very reverse.

That is called risking; and without risk faith is an impossibility. *To be related to spirit means to undergo a test;* to believe, to wish to believe, is to change one's life into a trial; daily test is the trial of faith. . . .

But where becoming a Christian is concerned there is, as compared with Socrates, a dialectical difference which must be remembered. Namely, where immortality is concerned man is only related to himself and to the idea, no further. But when a man chooses all at once to believe in Christ, i.e., chooses to stake his life upon him, he is allowed to have immediate (direct) recourse to Christ in prayer. Thus the historical is the cause, yet the object of faith.[158]

So we have come the full circle, returning to the beginning of the first chapter. For Kierkegaard, the existential relationship of contemporaneity to the historical Jesus is inseparable from his faith in the historical Jesus (in the first sense of the phrase) who lived, suffered, died, rose, ascended, and lives today.

III. Critique of Kierkegaard

Any critique of Kierkegaard must begin with an appreciation of the insight and incisiveness of his faith and thought.
It must also make the admission that the intimate correlation
of Kierkegaard's life and thought prohibits both the univer-
salizing of his experience and the squeezing of this existential thinker into the mold of our own day. What follows, then,
is an outline of some points which must be dealt with in any
contemporary utilization of Kierkegaard's approach to the
historical Jesus.

A. Methodological

1. An extreme Platonism is apparent in Kierkegaard's
metaphysic of finite/infinite. It is this which constitutes the
fundamental theological presupposition of Kierkegaard's
thought, i.e., the infinite qualitative difference between God
and man. It is this in turn which is responsible for intensi-
fying some of the problem areas for subsequent Christian
theology (including Kierkegaard's own theology), e.g., God
as the Unknown, the problem of revelation and reason, man
as created in the image of God, freedom versus grace, and,
most important, the "absurdity" of the incarnation (at least
as it is metaphysically depicted). By this presupposition
Kierkegaard subscribes to the formula *finitum non capax
infiniti;* but, if such categories are to be used at all, the

54

biblical writers and much subsequent philosophy and theology find it more congruous with Christian thought to say *infinitum capax finiti.*

2. Beyond this basic metaphysical presupposition, Kierkegaard adheres to no single philosophical system. He begins the "project of thought" in the *Fragments* in Socratic-Platonic (and generally idealistic) categories. In the "Interlude" of the same writing he portrays God in semi-Aristotelian terms. As the hypothetical work proceeds, however, Socrates recedes and Christ advances—Johannes Climacus "climbs" from philosophical to Christian categories. In the *Postscript* and *Training in Christianity* (the latter utilizing the opposite pseudonym, Anti-Climacus), Kierkegaard constructs existen·tial categories more appropriate to his own Christian expe· rience. And the fact that ultimately he comes "full circle' from the existential relationship of contemporaneity to the traditional understanding of the historical Jesus indicates that even the extreme Platonic metaphysic, which he has assumed to be fundamental, is rejected. Whatever the case, Kierkegaard illustrates the age-old search of Christian theology for a metaphysical system that can adequately contain it.

3. Utilizing the epistemology of the Greek skeptics, Kierkegaard asserts that immediate sensation and cognition cannot deceive. Error, like doubt, has its roots not in sensory perception but in the will, and can be overcome only by a corresponding affirmative act of the will, or direct faith. The skeptic, in holding his mind in suspense and not drawing conclusions from what is observed, can avoid the risk of error. Our contemporary insight into the subjective determinants of what a person perceives by means of the senses requires a correction of this understanding of the certitude which sensory perception gives.

4. The teleological category of "eternal happiness" is hardly adequate today, even for a discussion of the historical Jesus.

B. Biblical-Theological

1. Is the report, "that we have believed that in such and such a year the God appeared among us in the humble figure of a servant, that he lived and taught in our community, and finally died," really adequate for faith? Admittedly this is a hypothetical statement, since, as we have seen, Kierkegaard was convinced of the reliability of the testimony of the Gospels to the events of the life of Jesus. But even hypothetically—and more particularly in the light of biblical criticism from Wrede and Schweitzer to Bultmann and Fuchs—is this sufficient? Do we, can we, must we, have more than this as a historical basis for faith?

2. The resurrection is significantly absent from the statement just noted and is secondary, at least in explicit reference, in Kierkegaard's writings. Again granting the hypothetical nature of the report, the problem of the resurrection still remains both for Kierkegaard and for Christian discussion today. In the kerygma and the New Testament this event is of central importance and it continues to be an inescapable element in all biblical studies.

3. Considerable doubt is cast by biblical studies upon Kierkegaard's extreme assertion that Jesus said he was God. For Kierkegaard's purposes this conviction was true whether or not explicit self-testimony on the part of the historical Jesus could be located as a basis for it. But the problem of Christian teaching concerning Jesus Christ is neither avoided nor solved by the absence of such testimony, but is rather intensified.

4. What is the relationship between faith as the organ of the historical fact and faith as the organ of the absolute fact or of the existential relationship of contemporaneity to the historical Jesus? Can this single word (in English as in Danish) be used for both of these categories? More importantly, can these two concepts of faith be distinguished, as Kierkegaard seems to suggest in his hypothetical project, or are they not two aspects of the same act or leap of faith, even though the former is described as an act of the will and the latter as something for which God grants the condition?

5. Is it necessary, or even possible, to fix "an unshakable qualitative difference between the historical element in Christianity . . . and the history of Christianity"[159] as Kierkegaard does? How is this related to the doctrines of the Holy Spirit and the church, which are so neglected in Kierkegaard's thought?

Part II

Bultmann and the Quest of the Historical Jesus

IV. Bultmann and Kierkegaard and the Quest of the Historical Jesus

In previous chapters we have discussed Kierkegaard's understanding of the relationship of faith to the figure of Jesus of Nazareth. We noted primarily what we called "the existential relationship of contemporaneity with the historical Jesus"; but we suggested that for Kierkegaard personally this was inseparable from an essentially conservative attitude towards the events of Jesus' life as recorded in the four Gospels. To be contemporary with Jesus Christ was, to Kierkegaard, contingent upon the contemporaneity of the ascended Christ with us. Faith is subjectivity, but in dialectical relationship to the self-attesting authority of Christ.

We also described something of the philosophical, ecclesiastical, and personal situation in which Kierkegaard's thought developed, and pointed out that he thought of himself in this existential context as a "corrective," as one "without authority," "an existing individual." Contemporary thought has not always given heed to his warning against attempts to formulate an existentialist system from the fragments of his existential experience. Both directly and indirectly much of contemporary philosophy and theology is derivative from the insights of the "genius in a market-town."

Among the contemporary biblical scholars who have been

stimulated by Kierkegaard is Rudolf Bultmann. Philo-
sophically, by way of Heidegger, and theologically, by way
of the early "crisis" and "Word" theology of Karl Barth,
Kierkegaard has had no little influence on Bultmann's
thought. But it is particularly in Bultmann's hermeneutics,
especially with respect to history and the figure of Jesus,
that Kierkegaard's influence is apparent. Bultmann's work
began at the end of the nineteenth-century quest of the
historical Jesus. His opposition to that quest (and also to
contemporary efforts in the direction of a "new quest"[1])
rests in the Kierkegaardian antagonism to anything that
attempts to deny or replace the decision-character of faith.
To establish a historical basis for faith, be it of maximum
or minimum content, is to substitute knowledge for faith,
security for risk. "It is only when there is no such objective
guarantee that faith acquires meaning and strength, for only
then is it authentic decision."[2] In effect, Bultmann makes
a radical reaffirmation of the twin *foci* of Luther's theology:
the proclamation of the Gospel and justification by faith.
There can be no support for faith beyond the inner testimony of the Spirit. But faith is inescapably related to Jesus
Christ and the biblical testimony concerning him as it is
proclaimed by the preaching church. Combining the insights of the disciplines of form criticism and existentialist
theology,* Bultmann confronts a mid-twentieth-century version of the question Kierkegaard had faced a century earlier
and with which we are concerned: How is faith related to
historically uncertain facts?

*   *   *

In the previous chapter we suggested that any contemporary use of Kierkegaard's approach to the question of the
historical Jesus must deal with certain methodological and
biblical-theological points in his thought. This Bultmann

---

*Both of these matters will be dealt with in further detail.

does, at least indirectly; and we shall enter into his discussion of the subject at hand by way of the four methodological considerations.

First, we noted the extreme Platonism which underlies the fundamental presupposition of Kierkegaard's thought, the infinite qualitative difference between God and man. In Kierkegaard this conviction is present implicitly and as an explicit refutation of the Hegelian notion of the mediating function of reason overcoming the dichotomies—eternity/time, God/man, etc.* It is this presupposition which is the basis of his language regarding Jesus as the Absolute Paradox, the absurd, which offends our reason as well as our understanding of ourselves as naturally religious persons. But Kierkegaard's protest remained silent during the century which followed him, while religious immanentism and theism dominated European theology. Only with Barth's second edition of the *Römerbrief* was Kierkegaard's voice heard again proclaiming the infinite qualitative difference.

It is this same presupposition which informs the thought of Bultmann. Although he utilizes existentialist philosophy as the most appropriate form in which to understand and communicate the existential nature of faith today, this metaphysic of excessive Platonism underlies his position. God is "the transcendent God,"[3] "the hidden and mysterious . . . unknown God."[4] He is the Creator, but he is inaccessible in the world he has made. It is "wishful thinking to imagine the things of this world as a screen on which we view the transcendent and to hear in this world the rushing current of the divine lifestream."[5] God is the sovereign God of grace and judgment. He is not to be identified with any events in history**; he is the "God who stands aloof from the history of the nations."[6] Such language reflects a revised Platonism,

---

Supra, pp. 28-31.

**The distinction which Bultmann makes between "in history" and "within history" should be noted. Cf. *Existence and Faith*, p. 232.

affirming the transcendence of God, but not in spatial categories as traditional theology (including Kierkegaard's) assumed. God is transcendent in relation to man, *deus abscon-
ditus,* mysterious and unknown apart from faith. He is not,
however, apart from the earth or the universe, "up there"
or "out there." Nevertheless, the meaning of this fundamentally Platonic and Kierkegaardian principle remains.

Two corresponding negative and positive consequences
of this presupposition are basic to Bultmann's understanding
of history and faith. First, since God is transcendent, hidden
except to faith, there can be no objectifying of him or of
his action. To speak of God as an object is both meaningless
and self-contradictory. God cannot be immanently reduced
to some knowledge which is possessed once and for all
in a *Weltanschauung* such as pantheism,[7] or even in a Christian world view formulated upon an orthodox doctrine of
creation.[8] His transcendence cannot be adequately expressed
in the terminology of mysticism or idealistic thinking.[9] Nor
can God be made the object of logical proof or the answer
to theoretical questions raised by existentialist philosophers.[10]
And with particular reference to the contemporary stress
on biblical language regarding the "God who acts," Bultmann insists that "it is wrong to speak about God as acting
in general statements."[11] Speech about God has meaning
only when it is derived from its existential reference, i.e.,
from speaking simultaneously about myself as the person
who is existentially concerned and about God's action in
the concrete situation of my life which I experience "as the
encounter which demands my personal decision. . . . I cannot speak of God's action in general statements; I can only
speak of what he does here and now with me, of what he
speaks here and now to me."[12] The God "who stands aloof
from the history of the nations meets each man in his own
little history, his everyday life with its daily gifts and
demands."[13]

Since human life is lived out in time and space, man's encounter with God can only be a specific event here and now. This event, our being addressed by God here and now, our being questioned, judged, and blessed by him, is what we mean when we speak of an act of God.[14]

This is not to say that God has no existence apart from the believer or the act of believing; but his existence is a meaningless concept apart from the decision of faith.

Christian faith . . . believes that God acts upon us and addresses us in the specific here and now. . . . This kind of faith, however, is . . . an event occurring on specific occasions, and it can remain alive only when the believer is constantly asking himself what God is saying to him here and now. God is generally just as hidden for him as he is for everyone else. . . . What God is doing now—it is of course not to be identified *tout court* with the visible occurrence—I may not know as yet, and perhaps I shall never know. But still I must ask what he is trying to say to me through it, even if all he has to say is that I must just grin and bear it. . . . But this is just the paradox of faith: it understands an ascertainable event in its context in nature and history as the act of God. Faith cannot dispense with its "nevertheless."[15]

In Kierkegaard's language, truth—and faith—is subjectivity.[16]

There is also a positive consequence of this fundamental presupposition. Since God is qualitatively different from man, withdrawn from man's objective view but affirmed by decision in faith, all language about God and his acts must be in the categories knowable to all men, those of personal existence. God's action may be spoken of only in analogies drawn from the intimate communion between man and man. The existential experience of love, the contingencies of doubt and faith in human friendship, the caring and disciplining of fatherhood, the judgments and demands of personal life—all these are real experiences and may be considered as analogues (not symbols or images) of God's acting here and now.[17] "Only such statements about God are legitimate as express the existential relation between God and man. . . . The so-called images which describe God as acting are legitimate only if they mean that God is a personal being acting on persons."[18] Therefore all statements which speak of God's actions as cosmic events are illegitimate. Moreover, statements of the more familiar biblical type which describe God as acting in cultic, political, and juristic categories are inappropriate, except in a purely symbolic sense. Such mythological and cosmological language "objectifies the divine activity and projects it on the plane of worldly happenings."[19] This is the essence of myth: It expresses "the other-worldly in terms of this world and the divine in terms of human life, the other side in terms of this side."[20] It utilizes images not drawn from personal encounter. Therefore, to take seriously the transcendence of God which only faith can existentially affirm, we must demythologize the traditional concepts of theology. Only by demythologizing or deobjectifying this language about God, or, more adequately, only by reinterpreting it in terms of man's existential reference can "the true meaning of God's mystery, . . . how he acts with me,"[21] be maintained.

In his logical development of this second consequence of the fundamentally Kierkegaardian presupposition, Bultmann goes well beyond the thought of his predecessor. While Kierkegaard found existential language to be most appropriate for communicating the Christian faith, he did not seek to limit religious language to this category. Bultmann, on the other hand, moves within the frame of reference of existentialist philosophy as formulated in the early writings of Heidegger. Demythologizing is therefore primarily a consequence of this mode of thought and not just a matter of communicating the faith.*

---

*It should be noted in passing that Bultmann's usage of Heidegger's analysis of being is not intended to suggest that this is the true philosophical system for all time or even that theology must subscribe to Heidegger's philosophical theories. Rather, in the present historical situation, theology

The existential occasion for Bultmann's demand for de-mythologizing is not unrelated to the third point in the methodological conclusion to the discussion of Kierkegaard. We noted, in passing, Kierkegaard's acceptance of the cer-titude which immediate sensation and cognition give in con-trast to the uncertainty of historical facts and faith. Essen-tially this is the Kantian distinction between pure reason and practical reason. Bultmann assumes this distinction and sees it leading to potentially disastrous consequences for faith. The world of nature as perceived by the senses and under-stood by the natural sciences stands as a challenge to the view of the world in which faith is usually conveyed.

> Man's knowledge and mastery of the world have advanced to such an extent through science and technology that it is no longer possible for anyone seriously to hold the New Testament view of the world—in fact, there is no one who does.[22]

Modern man, who uses the consequences of science and technology, such is the electric light, radio, and contempo-rary surgical techniques, assumes that all of nature operates as a self-contained nexus of cause and effect which can be progressively apprehended if not controlled by the mind of

---

should be willing to learn from Heidegger's existentialist analysis and use it as the best philosophical preface to understanding today the New Testa-ment's self-understanding. Cf. *Kerygma and Myth*, II, p. 182. In this matter Bultmann essentially parallels Kierkegaard's willingness (noted in the second methodological conclusion above) to use or reject any metaphysical or philosophical system which seems appropriate at this moment for com-municating the Gospel. This further implies the freedom of theology to be constantly on the move. Just as man's self-understanding changes in dif-ferent historical contexts, so also the theologian's interpretation of the New Testament writings changes. The "theological thoughts of the New Testa-ment . . . can claim to have meaning for the present not as theoretical teachings, timeless general truths, but only as the expression of an under-standing of human existence which for the man of today also is a possibility for his understanding of himself—a possibility which is opened to him by the New Testament itself, in that it not only shows him that such self-understanding is the reply to the kerygma as the word of God addressing him, but also imparts to him the kerygma itself" (*Theology of the New Testament*, II, p. 251).

man. He "acknowledges as reality only such phenomena or events as are comprehensible within the framework of the rational order of the universe."[23] A three-storied universe, good and evil spirits, miracles and interferences with the laws of nature, events of resurrection and ascension, as well as Jewish apocalyptic mythology—all these reflect an obsolete view of the world. To maintain this mythological perspective in the midst of the modern scientific world-view is to invite inevitable conflict and disaster for faith. Add to this the gnostic myths of the pre-existence, incarnation, and exaltation of the Son of God, as well as the redemption of the world through him, and the Christian faith becomes incredible. Lest modern man reject the kerygma, the message of the church, because to his mind it has been identified with the antiquated and incomprehensible container in which it has been presented, the "deeper meaning which is concealed under the cover of mythology"[24] must be sought. That God encounters man in an existential demand for responsible decision is a skandalon that is disturbing enough to man. The false stumblingblocks created for modern man by an antiquated world-view must be cleared away.

Demythologizing, therefore, is demanded not only by the nature of that language which alone is adequate to speak of the transcendent God, but also by the existential concern for communicating the kerygma in a time when man's world-view and self-understanding have changed so radically. Only by reinterpreting the mythology will we "discover whether the New Testament offers man an understanding of himself which will challenge him to a genuine existential decision."[25] Hence the purpose of demythologizing is not "to make religion more acceptable to modern man by trimming the traditional biblical texts."[26] Rather, it is to deal with the fundamental hermeneutical problem of interpreting the Bible and the teachings of the church in such a way that faith can be nothing else but the response to the kerygma and that the kerygma is nothing else than God's word addressing man as a questioning and promising word, a condemning and forgiving word. As such a word it does not offer itself to critical thought but speaks to one's concrete existence.[27]

This, then, brings us to the fourth methodological conclusion of which we spoke previously. For Kierkegaard the question of the present relation of faith to past events is set in an eschatological reference: "Is it possible to base an eternal happiness upon historical knowledge?" As we have noted, Kierkegaard's language reflects his essential acceptance of the traditional world-view of the biblical writings Bultmann, on the other hand, rejects this particular eschatological interpretation as reflecting an obsolete world-view. It must be reinterpreted, therefore, in terms comprehensible to modern man. For Bultmann, this means the use of Heidegger's existentialist categories of self-understanding. The *eschaton* is not a future event but a present reality.[28] The "fullness of time" and the future eschatological event of the biblical language are to be identified with the eschatological event which happens here and now. The "moment" is not, as for Kierkegaard, the category for describing the encounter with God in the present as a believing contemporary with the past in such a way that it is determinative for a future "eternal happiness" beyond death. Rather, for Bultmann, the moment is essentially complete in itself, giving man freedom from the past—particularly from his own past (hence it is forgiveness), but also from past historical events —and giving him free openness for responsible historical action in the future in time.[29] The *telos* of Bultmann's theology is not a future life at the end of chronological time (be it of world history or of my own history), but "authentic being,"[30] in the now when "God's action bestows upon us a new understanding of ourselves."[31]

. . . *the meaning in history lies always in the present,* and when the present is conceived as the eschatological present by Christian faith the meaning in history is realised. Man who complains: "I cannot see meaning in history, and therefore my life, interwoven in history, is meaningless," is to be admonished: do not look around yourself into universal history, you must look into your own personal history. Always in your present lies the meaning in history, and you cannot see it as a spectator, but only in your responsible decisions. In every moment slumbers the possibility of being the eschatological moment. You must awaken it.[32]

What, then, is the relation of these methodological procedures to the question at hand regarding Bultmann's understanding of faith and the historical Jesus *vis-à-vis* that of Kierkegaard? Quite evidently, from what has been indicated, any relationship of faith to the historical Jesus must, for Bultmann, be in terms corresponding to Kierkegaard's category of "the existential relation of contemporaneity." In our analysis of Kierkegaard on this point we noted the way in which he perceived the problem of certitude in history.* Factual certainty regarding the events in Jesus' life, the *what* of his life, is equally possible for eyewitnesses of the events and for subsequent generations by means of the reports of the eyewitnesses. But the *that* of Jesus' life, that he actually existed as a historical person—this demands a leap of (direct) faith. Only by the affirmation of the will in the face of uncertainty can we be historically contemporaneous with Jesus. Historical fact gives only approximation; faith holds fast to the objective uncertainty in the passion of inwardness.

Bultmann essentially reverses these two aspects of what Kierkegaard called "the historical fact." *That* Jesus existed —a reality uncertain apart from faith to Kierkegaard—is to Bultmann no problem:

Of course the doubt as to whether Jesus really existed is unfounded and not worth refutation. No sane person can doubt that Jesus stands

---

Supra, pp. 36-42.

as the founder behind the historical movement whose first distinct stage is represented by the oldest Palestinian community. . . . By the tradition Jesus is named as bearer of the message; according to overwhelming probability he really was. Should it prove otherwise, that does not change in any way what is said in the record. I see then no objection to naming Jesus throughout [this book, *Jesus and the Word*] as the speaker. Whoever prefers to put the name of "Jesus" always in quotation marks,** and let it stand as an abbreviation for the historical phenomenon with which we are concerned, is free to do so.[33]

"The decisive thing is simply the 'that.' "[34]

The *what* of Jesus' life, however—what Kierkegaard accepted as historically certain, i.e., the basic credibility of the accounts in the four Gospels—has been shattered by a century of biblical studies, typified by Strauss (the distinction between the Synoptic Gospels and the Fourth Gospel as sources), Wrede (the discovery that Mark's interpretive theory of the messianic secret destroys confidence in the earliest Gospel's objective history), Schweitzer (the radical eschatology apparent in Jesus' own teaching), and Harnack (the transformation of the Gospel through the process of Hellenizing within the church).

Even more decisive is the fact that *Formgeschichte* studies have demonstrated that the Synoptic Gospels are not in any way to be understood as historical-biographical documents, but as testimonies of faith. Bultmann identifies three strands of material in the present Gospels.[35] Some of the most ancient Aramaic tradition may possibly go back to Jesus himself, particularly the more obscure portions of his teachings which do not reflect subsequent Christian interpretation in either Jewish eschatological or Hellenistic mythological categories. We do "know enough of his message to mark for ourselves a consistent picture, . . . though it can be marked off with only relative exactness."[36] Fundamentally it was an eschatological-ethical message, proclaimed within the context of the Jewish apocalyptic hope.[37] The dominant theme

---

*Bultmann himself does not follow this procedure, however.

is the proclamation that the reign of God is at hand. The old aeon is rapidly approaching its end; the new aeon will dawn immanently with terror and tribulation, brought as a miraculous event by God alone. Meanwhile the signs of the inruption of God's new time are to be found in Jesus' own presence and deeds and message which call men to decision before the coming of the Son of Man to judge the earth. The indicative implies an imperative: repent and obey. In contrast to the formal obedience required by Jewish legalism, the breaking-in of the new age demands the radical obedience of man's total life to the demand for love. In effect, then, Jesus appeared as a messianic prophet with a unique consciousness of his own authority in preparing for the impending victorious reign of God.

Regarding Jesus himself, however, considerably less can be said with any certainty.

We must frankly confess that the character of Jesus as a human personality cannot be recovered by us. We can neither write a "life of Jesus" nor present an accurate picture of his personality. Even in regard to the question of his messianic consciousness we seem compelled to admit ignorance.[38]

With some caution, the following things regarding Jesus' activity may be affirmed: his exorcisms, his antagonism to Jewish legalism as evidenced by his violation of Sabbath regulations and abandonment of ritual purification, his fraternizing with social and moral outcasts, his sympathy for women and children, his lack of asceticism, and the calling of disciples and followers.[39] The one certain fact in his life is that he was crucified by the Romans and thus suffered the death of a political criminal. Beyond this we cannot go. "The greatest embarrassment to the attempt to reconstruct a portrait of Jesus is the fact that we cannot know how Jesus understood his end, his death."[40] Thus the life-of-Jesus research has failed to rescue from the fire something that may be relevant for faith. The only incontestable fact is the *that* of the life of Jesus of Nazareth and his crucifixion.*

The second strand of material in the Gospels which *Formgeschichte* studies can isolate with considerable confidence is constituted by the kerygma—the message or proclamation—which arose within the life of the primitive church. Only after the death of the historical Jesus could the preaching about the victorious Christ begin. "He who formerly had been the *bearer* of the message was drawn into it and became its essential *content. The proclaimer became the proclaimed.*"[41] The Christ of the kerygma displaced the historical Jesus. What was proclaimed by the church was not historical facts, but the Easter faith regarding the Christ. Jesus of Nazareth, the Teacher and Prophet, was interpreted and proclaimed in categories understandable within the eschatological congregation in Palestine—as the Messiah and the Son of Man. Subsequently in Hellenistic Christianity the kerygma was reformulated in the language of gnostic mythology. It was this kerygma of the Hellenistic church that won Paul to the Christian faith and which he in turn brought to further theological clarity. The daily life of the church at the same time demanded resources for its own edification and prophecy as well as for apologetic and polemic purposes. These practical needs led to the production and collection of sayings of Jesus (culminating in the Q source presupposed by the parallel material in Matthew and Luke) and of narratives of miracles and Passion events. As the Hellenistic church took over the Palestinian tradition, other requirements within the church shaped the traditional material into early forms of Gospels, such as Mark. The appearance of these uniquely Christian documents, the Gospels, marks the third strand of material. The evangelists edited previous oral and written traditions within the life of particular congrega-

---

*Cf. Kierkegaard's hypothetical report, *supra*, p. 46.

tions. The Synoptic Gospels are not literary documents existing on their own, but are "completely subordinate to Christian faith and worship."[42] Similarly, the author of the Fourth Gospel adapted the kerygmatic traditions in another direction of Hellenistic thought by portraying Jesus as the gnostic Revealer. But in every instance what was proclaimed and written regarding the Christ was preserved and interpreted within the *Sitz im Leben* of the early church. All these materials constitute the kerygma in the broadest sense, the word of God's act in the Christ, the living Lord of the church.

Bultmann emphasizes the difference between the historical Jesus and the Christ of the kerygma of the early church. Fundamentally, the distinction is threefold.[43] First, in the kerygma the mythical form of the Son of God takes the place of the historical person of Jesus of Nazareth. Second, in the kerygma (including Paul and John) the eschatological event is not primarily future, as it was in the proclamation of Jesus, but it is proclaimed as having already occurred in the vicarious death of Jesus for the sins of men and in God's miraculous raising of him from the dead. Third, confessional formulations about Jesus Christ assume the priority over Jesus' message of the call to the radical obedience of love: The imperative takes second place to the indicative.

Relating this to Kierkegaard, it may be said that what he demanded of the Hegelians and knew well himself—that man is never an objective spectator but an existing individual —he failed to apply to the authors of the biblical sources, since he accepted their fundamental historical credibility. Bultmann, however, for both scholarly and existential reasons, essentially reaffirms Schweitzer's eulogy at the end of the nineteenth-century quest of the historical Jesus.* That quest is today both impossible and illegitimate.[44] But with

---

Supra, pp. 10-11.

Kierkegaard he can affirm regarding the relationship of faith and historical facts:

The kerygma is not interested in the "objective historicity" beyond that "that," but requires faith in the crucified and risen Christ. . . . [But] faith does not at all arise from the acceptance of historical facts. . . . Of what use then is historical legitimization? . . . The historical-critical analysis of the Synoptic Gospels which inquires into the objectively ascertainable history of Jesus suffices only to corroborate the "that" which the kerygma maintains in the face of a possible skepticism regarding Jesus' historicity, and to illustrate it with a degree of probability.[45]

To put it another way, the Christian theologian is not interested in reconstruction, but in interpretation, just as were the authors of the New Testament. The writings of the canon are not to be interrogated as sources which the historian interprets in order to reconstruct a picture of primitive Chistianity as a phenomenon of the past. Rather, whatever reconstruction may be attempted "stands in the service of the interpretation of the New Testament writings under the presupposition that they have something to say to the present."[46]

Does this imply an end of the relationship between the Jesus of history and faith? Bultmann answers this in two ways. First, while there is a discrepancy between the historical Jesus and the Christ of the kerygma, there is continuity between the historical Jesus and the kerygma itself. The kerygma, including the formulations of Paul and John, presupposes the historical Jesus. All the oral and written traditions require the *that* of Jesus' life as well as the fact of his crucifixion. But beyond this, nothing more is necessary.

Secondly, Bultmann's existentialist hermeneutic of history gives a more fundamental answer. Since, in Kierkegaard's categories, we are not living in a parenthesis, but are existing individuals living within history and having our own history, our interest in history is for more than information on interesting occurrences in the past, more than a walk through a museum of antiquities. . . . It is really to lead to our seeing Jesus as a part of the history in which we have our being. . . . [It] must be in the nature of a continuous *dialogue with history*. Further, it should be understood that the dialogue does not come as a conclusion, as a kind of evaluation of history after one has first learned the objective facts. On the contrary, the actual encounter with history takes place only in the dialogue. We do not stand outside historical forces as neutral observers; we are ourselves moved by them; and only when we are ready to listen to the *demand* which history makes on us do we understand at all what history is all about. This dialogue is no clever exercise of subjectivity on the observer's part, but a real *interrogating* of history, in the course of which the historian puts this subjectivity of his in question, and is ready to listen to history as an authority. . . . History, however, does not speak when a man stops his ears, that is, when he assumes neutrality, but speaks only when he comes seeking answers to the questions which agitate him. Only by this attitude can we discover whether an objective element is really present in history and whether history has something to say to us. . . . We ourselves, standing in the current of history, can gain clear insight into the contingencies and necessaries of our own life purpose.[47]

Thus while Kierkegaard allows discussion of "the objective problem" of the historical fact of Jesus of Nazareth, Bultmann essentially rejects it. The cause of this difference is the divergent attitudes towards objective history held by these two existentialist thinkers. Kierkegaard, living at the inception of the movement of objective historiography, was willing to acknowlege the validity of a concern for historical facts. He had to insist, however, that the mere possession of such facts, even when combined with the affirmation of the *that* of Jesus' existence, does not make one a disciple. Bultmann, on the other hand, living at a time when the perversions of objective history *(Historie*)* had become apparent, pursues meaningful history *(Geschichte**)*, past history which has an existential reference to our lives today. This

---

Historie=objective history; *historisch*=historical.
**Geschichte=meaningful history; *geschichtlich*=historic.

perspective is not concerned with the certitude of facts per se, but with

facts of the past [which] become historical phenomena when they become significant for a subject which itself stands in history and is involved in it; only then they have something to say; and that they only do for the subject which comprehends them. . . . The most subjective understanding . . . is the most objective; only those stirred by the question of their own existence can hear the claim the text makes.[48]

The fundamental and essential presupposition in this existentialist hermeneutic of *Geschichte* is the historian's "life-relation"[49] with the subject matter. A hermeneutic without presuppositions is impossible. Every interpreter has an implicit or explicit "pre-understanding" of man and his possibilities which he brings to his reading of a text. In this respect there is no special hermeneutic for the study of the Bible, as compared with other documents. Methodological study requires that the interpreter have an "existential rapport with the subject in the text he is trying to interpret."[50] The (existentialist) biblical interpreter moves from the situation of his own life into that of the biblical authors, asking the question which arises from the depths of his own existence and which he discovers arising in them as well: What must I do to be saved? This dialogue with history is a continuing circle, the "hermeneutical circle." In the historicity of a human being, his pre-understanding is confronted by the preaching of the kerygma which demands that he

decide on a new understanding of myself as free from myself by the grace of God and as endowed with my new self, and . . . accept a new life grounded in the grace of God. In making this decision I also decide on a new understanding of my responsible acting.[51]

Encounter, demand, and decision constitute the "eschatological event."

Summarizing, then, a double approach to Jesus is apparent

in Bultmann, roughly corresponding to Kierkegaard's "historical fact" and "absolute fact." On the one hand, Jesus of Nazareth is the human historical person (Kierkegaard: the historical fact) who as an event in *Historie* "provides the condition" (Kierkegaard: "serves as an occasion") for the church's proclamation of the kerygma "on each specific occasion."[52] This human figure is exposed to the objective observation of the historian, but the consequences of historical study for faith are nil. (Kierkegaard: "Faith cannot be distilled from even the nicest accuracy of detail.") On the other hand, the church's proclamation of the kerygma did not originate in the historical *(historisch)* statements or events of Jesus' life. It was inaugurated by the eschatological event in which "the proclaimer became the proclaimed."[53] This kerygmatic event of Jesus Christ—the Christ of the kerygma (Kierkegaard: the absolute fact)—is apprehended only in one's own historic *(geschichtlich)* encounter with the "saving event" (Kierkegaard: the Absolute Paradox) which demands decision.

> The eschatological event which is Jesus Christ happens here and now as the Word is being proclaimed. . . . Thus, the "once-for-all" is now understood in its genuine sense, namely, as the "once-for-all" of the eschatological event. For this "once-for-all" is not the uniqueness of an historical event, but means that a particular historical event, that is Jesus Christ, is to be understood as the eschatological "once-for-all." As an eschatological event this "once-for-all" is always present in the proclaimed word, not as a timeless truth. . . . It is the eschatological "once-for-all" because the word becomes event here and now.[54]

Thus the word that is proclaimed about Jesus Christ and the victory of God's redemption meets a man in the situation of his own life as an encounter, a demand, and a decision. The past becomes a living present, encountering him as a living word, providing grace, and demanding the radical obedience of love.

❊   ❊   ❊

At this point the decisive difference between Kierkegaard and Bultmann is beginning to become apparent; but an examination of three aspects of Jesus' life which are crucial for faith should make it quite clear.

First, the event of the cross. Bultmann, like Kierkegaard in his hypothetical report, deems this event as the one certain historical fact in Jesus' life, even though the details are obscured behind the sources of the Scriptures. But contemporary biblical studies have demonstrated that one further thing "is then certain. . . . Jesus did not speak of his death . . . as [a] redemptive act."[55] The process of mythological interpretation of his death in cosmic, juridicial, and sacrificial terms began within the church as it sought to convey the significance of this event. These mythological categories portray the crucifixion as a fact of history which affects mankind in general, so that the individual may rely upon it for forgiveness and salvation. "In this the church is wrong."[56] In Bultmann's carefully chosen words:

To believe in the cross of Christ does not mean to concern ourselves with a mythical process wrought outside of us and our world, with an objective event turned by God to our advantage, but rather to make the cross of Christ our own, to undergo crucifixion with him. . . . In other words, the cross is not just an event of the past which can be contemplated, but is the eschatological event in and beyond time, in so far as it (understood in its significance, that is, for faith) is an ever-present reality. . . .

In its redemptive aspect the cross of Christ is no mere mythical event, but a historic *(geschichtlich)* fact originating in the historical *(historisch)* event which is the crucifixion of Jesus. The abiding significance of the cross is that it is the judgment of the world, the judgment and deliverance of man. So far as this is so, Christ is crucified "for us." . . . The historical *(historisch)* event of the cross has, in the significance peculiar to it, created a new historic *(geschichtlich)* situation. The preaching of the cross as the event of redemption challenges all who hear it to appropriate this significance for themselves, to be willing to be crucified with Christ

But, it will be asked, is this significance to be discerned in the actual event of past history? Can it, so to speak, be read off from that event? Or does the cross bear this significance because it is the cross

of *Christ?* In other words, must we first be convinced of the significance of Christ and believe in him in order to discern the real meaning
of the cross? If we are to perceive the real meaning of the cross, must
we understand it as the cross of Jesus as a figure of past history?
Must we go back to the Jesus of history?

As far as the first preachers of the gospel are concerned this will
certainly be the case. . . . But for us this personal connection cannot
be reproduced. For us the cross cannot disclose its own meaning: it is
an event of the past. We can never recover it as an event in our
own lives.[57]

Secondly, the resurrection. Here, Bultmann says, we are
dealing with something quite different from the cross. While
the cross is a historical event which to faith becomes a historic, saving fact, essentially the opposite is true of the resurrection. A saving fact produces, as it were, a historical fact
in the mind of the disciples. This, admittedly, is not the way
the New Testament portrays the resurrection. "The resurrection of Jesus is often used in the New Testament as a
miraculous proof"[58] for the faith of the church. In 1 Corinthi-
ans 15, for example, Paul adduces a list of eyewitnesses to the
miracle of the resurrection. Actually, however, the eyewitnesses "guarantee St. Paul's preaching, not the fact of the
resurrection. An historical fact which involves a resurrection
from the dead is utterly inconceivable!"[59] In other words, the
disciples did not proclaim the risen Christ because they
found the tomb empty or because Jesus appeared to them.
Such stories are legendary embellishments of the primitive
tradition. Rather they preached the resurrection because
they had come to believe in Christ as their risen Lord. They
were "united with him in his resurrection."[60] Hence the resurrection is an article of faith, not a historical fact or an
incredible mythological event like the resuscitation of a
corpse. If the resurrection is to be attached to any historical
event, it is "firmly rooted to the earthly figure of the crucified
Jesus."[61] Only as such is it the eschatological event *par excellence*. Again, in Bultmann's words:

In this way the resurrection is not a mythological event adduced in order to prove the saving efficacy of the cross, but an article of faith just as much as the meaning of the cross itself. Indeed, *faith in the resurrection is really the same thing as faith in the saving efficacy of the cross,* faith in the cross as the cross of Christ. Hence you cannot first believe in Christ and then in the strength of that faith believe in the cross. To believe in Christ means to believe in the cross as the cross of Christ. The saving efficacy of the cross is not derived from the fact that it is the cross of Christ: it is the cross of Christ because it has this saving efficacy. Without that efficacy it is the tragic end of a great man.

The real Easter faith is faith in the word of preaching which brings illumination. If the event of Easter Day is in any sense an historical event additional to the event of the cross, it is nothing else than the *rise of faith in the risen Lord,* since it was this faith which led to the apostolic preaching. The resurrection itself is not an event of past history. All that historical criticism can establish is the fact that the first disciples came to believe in the resurrection. . . . But the historical problem is not of interest to Christian belief in the resurrection. For the historical event of the rise of the Easter faith means for us what it meant for the first disciples—namely, the self-attestation of the risen Lord, the act of God in which the redemptive event of the cross is completed. . . .

This word [of reconciliation within the church's proclamation] supplements the cross and makes its saving efficacy intelligible by demanding faith and confronting men with the question whether they are willing to understand themselves as men who are crucified and risen with Christ.[62]

In this respect the contemporary Christian is no different from Paul. The kerygma of the Hellenistic church confronted him with the decision of regarding the crucified Jesus of Nazareth, whom the kerygma claimed to be raised from the dead, as the Messiah. This meant a decision regarding the crucifixion of Christ as a judgment upon his self-understanding up to that time. This he had rejected as a persecutor of the church. But in his conversion he surrendered his previous self-understanding, sacrificed what had given meaning and pride to his life, i.e., obedience to the law, and accepted God's judgment on all his accomplishments and boasting. Thus his old self was crucified with Christ; in Christ he became a new creature.[63]

Third, what about that which to Kierkegaard was the heart of the absurdity of the Absolute Paradox, "He said . . . that he was God"? Bultmann portrays Jesus of Nazareth as the eschatological-ethical prophet, as we have noted above. Only after the resurrection was the bearer of the message transformed into its content. "The proclaimer became the proclaimed." After this eschatological event the church read back into the life of Jesus Jewish messianic motifs and Hellenistic redemption myths. The passages in the Gospels which appear to be messianic or redemptive are *vaticinia ex eventu*. The oldest tradition "reveals no trace of a consciousness on his [Jesus'] part of being the Servant of God,"[64] or the Messiah,[65] or the Son of Man.[66] More significantly, the stories in the Gospels portraying Jesus as the Son of God (particularly the Baptism and transfiguration accounts) are either legends or Easter stories projected backwards.

Bultmann uses a similar approach in interpreting other New Testament passages which speak of Jesus in language which has given rise to creedal affirmations such as that of the World Council of Churches which confesses "Jesus Christ as God and Savior." The decisive question is whether such statements are intended to express the "nature" *(physis)* of Christ or to speak of *Christus pro me*.

The formula, "Christ is God," is false in every sense in which "God" is understood as an entity which can be objectivized. . . . It is correct if "God" is understood here as the event of God's acting [here and now]. . . . Revelation occurs in a concrete historical man and is renewed at any given time in the preaching of concrete historical men who preach Christ as my God.[67]

Again, more precisely regarding the relationship of the Christ-kerygma to the historical Jesus, Bultmann says:

We can hope . . . to recognize the historical phenomenon "Jesus" only on the basis of one's own historic *(geschichtlich)* encounter. . . .
The Jesus of history is not kerygma. . . . For in the kerygma Jesus encounters us as the Christ—that is, as the eschatological phenomenon

par excellence. Neither St. Paul nor St. John mediate an historic encounter with the historic Jesus. . . . To understand Jesus as the
eschatological phenomenon (that is, as the Savior through whom God
delivers the world by passing judgement on it and granting the future
as a gift to those who believe in him), all that is necessary is to proclaim that he has come. . . .

. . . I am deliberately renouncing any form of encounter with a
phenomenon of past history, including an encounter with the Christ
after the flesh, in order to encounter the Christ proclaimed in the
kerygma, which confronts me in my historic situation.[68]

These illustrations from Jesus' life and particularly these
last words clearly define the difference between Kierkegaard
and Bultmann regarding the relationship of faith and the
historical Jesus. While they concur in many respects regarding the minimal role that objective facts may have for
faith and also in their common existential concern and language, they differ greatly on the content, i.e., the theological
and interpretive content, of both the historical event and
the kerygmatic event. Very simply, they diverge in their
understanding of Jesus Christ. This may be seen in two
ways.

First, quite obviously they differ regarding the interpretation of who Jesus of Nazareth was. To Kierkegaard, he was
the Absolute Paradox, the Servant-Savior-Teacher. He was
God incarnate. *This* is the offense, both to reason and to our
self-understanding as inherently religious persons. For Bultmann, this account of "the transcendence of God . . . reduced to immanence"[69] is a myth. Like all the accompanying
myths it must be demythologized or reinterpreted so that
what appears to be an offense or *skandalon* will be properly
understood and dismissed as a *false skandalon.* "Instead we
have the true paradox of a transcendent God present and
active in history: 'The Word became flesh.' "[70] "The *eschaton*
has actually entered history."[71] This is the *real skandalon.*
It is not the *skandalon* of Jesus of Nazareth who was God.
Rather it is God's activity here and now which is the *skandalon* to modern man just as it was in the days of Jesus.

Secondly, for Kierkegaard there is a continuity in person between the historical fact, Jesus of Nazareth, and the absolute fact who confronts us today. This continuity is by way of the resurrection (which, as we have noted, Kierkegaard assumes, although he gives little explicit attention to it) and the ascension. Jesus Christ was a historical fact and is a living Lord. Immediate contemporaneity with the historical fact of the past is impossible. But faith provides contemporaneity, not with the historical fact, however, but with the historical fact who became the living Christ through the resurrection and the ascension—Jesus Christ the man. And he, the risen man, Jesus Christ, is contemporaneous with the believer. For Bultmann, however, there is a discontinuity in person between Jesus of Nazareth and the eschatological event which is called Jesus Christ, i.e., the Christ of the kerygma. This discontinuity arises because Jesus of Nazareth is dead (although Bultmann never states this in so many words). Neither immediate contemporaneity nor historical contemporaneity is possible with Jesus of Nazareth. Faith has no interest in Christ after the flesh, i.e., the man Jesus. Rather it is faith in the kerygma which tells of God's dealings in Jesus of Nazareth. What encounters us today is not Jesus of Nazareth, but the kerygma, the word of God which is preached through a human mouth within the church and which meets with either faith or unbelief. With this kerygma we have an existential contemporaneity. God speaks directly to me, here and now, summoning me to my true humanity. This is revelation—to me. This event—God speaking to me—is God's way of acting today. This speech-event is the eschatological event. This is what is called in theology "Jesus Christ." It is this living word of God which has continuity with the act of God in Jesus of Nazareth and in which he may be said to be really present today. "To believe in the Christ present in the kerygma is the meaning of the Easter faith."[72]

V. Critique of Bultmann

In our analysis of Bultmann's thought, we indicated how he shares a common point of departure with Kierkegaard. Along the way there are frequent meeting points and approximations in their understanding of the relationship of faith and the historical event of Jesus of Nazareth. Toward the end of the study, however, it has become apparent that there are major discrepancies and basic contradictions. This is as it should be. As we stated in the critique of Kierkegaard, it would be against the spirit of his own self-understanding as a "corrective" to universalize his point of view or to insist that it apply to the changed circumstances of another age. In addition, since Kierkegaard's day there has been a general acceptance of some fundamental scholarly conclusions regarding the development of the Christian tradition and Scriptures within the life of the early Christian church. Although the details of this process have been variously developed in the century of biblical studies since Kierkegaard, it is simply impossible to ignore or reject the basic insights and return to a precritical traditional position. Kierkegaard's existentialist methodology was for him inseparable from his biblical and theological orthodoxy: We noted how he came "full circle" from the existential relationship of contemporaneity to the traditional picture of the historical Jesus who lived, died, rose, ascended, and lives today. Contemporary theology and hermeneutics have sought to separate these, preserving and refining the existentialist insights which have become quite determinative in our age and discarding the traditional frame of reference which is no longer tenable. As we have seen, Bultmann has been a leading figure in this process.

Any critique of Bultmann demands a recognition of the positive contribution he has made in this area of thought. He, above all, has been responsible for putting the hermeneutical problem in the central place where it belongs. Biblical studies and theology have both too often pursued their particular and esoteric interests, not only in isolation from each other, but also without raising the fundamental question of methodology and interpretation. However one may evaluate Bultmann's hermeneutic, it must be admitted that he has raised the question in inescapable fashion, and neither biblical studies nor theology can ignore it.

Secondly, Bultmann has extended Kierkegaard's concern for the decision-character of faith even further than his predecessor. He seeks to avoid completely the subject-object distinction found in the older epistemology and theology and still apparent even in Kierkegaard. The hermeneutical circle is the clearest symbol of existentialist methodology. *Wort–Antwort–Verantwort*—the circle remains unbroken. Word, response, and responsibility are inseparable from one another. There is no possibility of speaking a true word about God in any context other than that of the involvement of faith. The concept of the divine is meaningless apart from faith. Likewise there is no objective revelation, no objective word from the beyond. The "object of faith" is not given to the historian; the "Subject" of faith is known only in the existential situation of another subject. As we indicated in introducing Bultmann, the twin, hence inseparable, *foci* of Luther's theology are radically reaffirmed by Bultmann. The word of God is a creative and judging power, proclaimed within the worshiping congregation.* It is through the kerygma, the proclamation by a human being, that God acts here and now. This is inseparable from the historical figure of Jesus and the biblical testimonies to him, but it is not a word about the past. There is no false contemporaneity with ancient events, no historicism so typical of both pietism and moralism, no biblicism. The word is a living, active word to me. Hence the word is inseparable from faith. Faith can find no security for itself. It cannot rest in proofs for the existence of God, in true doctrine, in an infallible book or church, or even in subjectivism. Faith is a personal decision for responsible action in response to a word spoken to me in my situation. Man is justified by faith in and through the word of God.

Next, Bultmann has correctly focused upon the crucial nature of the crucifixion-resurrection event as the decisive event in Christian history. This is the prism through which were interpreted prior events in Jesus' life; this is the determinative category for the Christian's life. Faith is not dependent upon historical facticity regarding the events of Jesus' life or his teaching. The Christian faith is an Easter faith; it proclaims the risen Lord who demands that we be crucified and rise with him.

Finally, Bultmann has sought to take seriously the fact that the interpreter is within history and has his own history. The Christian faith can be understood only within the context of man's current view of the world. The obsolete *Weltanschauung* which assumed the existence of two worlds must be discarded. Contemporary natural science prohibits the division of space into two (or three) spheres. Similarly an antiquated metaphysic which divides reality into two realms must be avoided as must a theology which speaks of

---

*Bultmann's stress upon the proclaimed word within the worshiping congregation is in sharp contrast to Kierkegaard's relative deemphasis upon the church as a worshiping community.

an eternal *Heilsgeschichte* or *Urgeschichte* apart from temporal history. The consequence is for Bultmann a radical historicization of mankind and of the Christian faith. God and man are properly understood only within the context of human history and a man's particular history. Theological language must be adequately reinterpreted lest modern man be obliged to have faith only at the sacrifice of his intellect. To his credit, Bultmann seeks to reinterpret faith in what appears to him to be the most adequate contemporary language, Heidegger's early phenomenological analysis of being with its stress upon man's continuing quest for authentic existence. This existentialist philosophy replaces various forms of Platonism or other world views as a proper preface to the self-understanding of man derived from the encounter with the kerygma.

❊   ❊   ❊

It is at this point, however, that several questions must be raised regarding Bultmann's methodology and approach to the problem at hand.

1. Certain problems arise in connection with Bultmann's understanding of myth. Normally the term is used in a religious and philosophical sense to refer to any objectifying of God and his actions in cosmic, cultic, or apocalyptic categories. Such accounts must be demythologized or, as Bultmann clarifies, reinterpreted in existentialist categories of personal relationships. In this manner they become analogues, not literal or mythological statements; but as such they are adequate to describe the relation between God and man. On the other hand, there is another way in which the word "myth" is used in a purely pejorative sense. This is to refer to stories that are incapable of remythologization because they are too intimately associated with an obsolete scientific world view. These myths are false, according to Bultmann, and must simply be discarded. But the question

arises, What is the clear criterion for distinguishing between these two types of myth? Even more fundamentally, can the Christian experience of faith be adequately contained in nonmythological language? Are such categories of necessity synonymous with objectifying? Is it not possible—and necessary—to continue the use of the politically oriented mythological language of the Bible by rejecting a literalistic scientific interpretation (e.g., a three-story universe, the account of creation, Christ's miracles and physical resuscitation-resurrection, the end of the world), yet maintaining the meaningful, symbolic character of the myth? Do not the myths need to be deobjectified, deliteralized, rather than, as Bultmann suggests, either reinterpreted in existentialist categories (which constitute their own type of mythological language) or rejected *en toto?* A further question arises in this connection. Does not Bultmann's understanding of the metaphysical, philosophical, theological, and historical implications of "modern science" go considerably beyond what scientists and philosophers of science themselves would claim? Is not the category "modern science" extremely ambiguous and actually, in Bultmann's use, more akin to an antiquated (though still popular) view of science more appropriately called scientism?

2. Bultmann removes God from the realm of space to the realm of history. History in turn is included within the epistemology of pure reason and subjected to interpretation as a nexus of cause and effect. Hence the resurrection, for example, is rendered incredible according to the canons of natural science. Is there not the necessity, as Richard R. Niebuhr suggests,[73] of formulating and accepting a discipline of historical reason, distinct from both metaphysics and natural science, which will interpret history on its own terms? The quality of repeatability and regularity which is so important in some areas of natural science is the

exact opposite of the quality of uniqueness and unrepeatability that is basic to historical meaning.

3. Bultmann seems to retreat not only from the metaphysical to the historical, but from the historical to the existentialist realm of existence. He moves from space to time to the self. While history is given a central position as the realm of God's activity, ultimately past history is swallowed up in the present. The historical Jesus has no fundamental place in contemporary faith. Even the kerygma is dehistoricized. Thus Kierkegaard's neglect of the doctrine of the Spirit within the past history of the church is intensified. Ultimately Jesus and the ancient kerygma concerning him are replaced by the living Spirit in the presently proclaimed kerygmatic word, and human history, as well as *Heilsgeschichte*, is replaced by the individual's own history, his personal *Heilsgeschichte*. In spite of Bultmann's insistence upon responsible action within history, both faith and responsibility are depicted primarily in the personalistic way reminiscent of older forms of pietism. The consequence is a form of *fideism*, in which faith is unambiguously central, but the "other side" of faith—grace—is radically peripheral.

4. Bultmann's well-intentioned use of the early Heidegger to understand and communicate the kerygma inevitably recreates the problem noted previously regarding Kierkegaard, that of the adequacy of any philosophical framework or preface for the Christian faith. Heidegger's own thought has gone beyond the phenomenological analysis of human existence found in *Being and Time*. Bultmann's thought is so closely identified with this passing philosophical position that it ironically runs the risk of becoming an esoteric methodology and language that is no longer acceptable by philosophy and is rejected by much theology. Bultmann ultimately ends up speaking to "Bultmannians."

5. Bultmann utilizes the conclusions of *Formgeschichte* studies regarding the crucial nature of the complex of events associated with the crucifixion, resurrection, and the giving of the Spirit. These constitute the prism through which earlier events in Jesus' life are interpreted by faith. Also, these studies indicate that the faith of the early church was above all in the living, present Lord. Bultmann thus seeks to avoid the "Jesiolatry" and hero-worship apparent in much of orthodoxy, pietism, and moralism. He has no interest in "Christ after the flesh." The fundamental question arises, however, as to whether Bultmann does not overstress the discontinuity between Jesus of Nazareth and the Christ-kerygma. The kerygma proclaimed not only the living Lord, but the living Lord who had lived and died in the midst of men. In spite of Bultmann's rejoinders, is there not a greater continuity between the historical Jesus and the Christ of the kerygma? Does not the relationship of the kerygma to the historical Jesus extend to more than the *that?* Does it not also include more of the *what* than Bultmann allows, particularly in the area of Jesus' words and deeds as they reflect his own understanding of himself (as the proponents of the "new quest" suggest)? In other words, is there not a kerygmatic message of the church latent, if not apparent, in Jesus' own words and deeds, even though the determinative event for the church's kerygma is the Easter event? Also, in this connection, the question of "what happened?" in the events associated with the Easter faith continues to fascinate and disturb the Christian mind, even though the details of the event may be lost forever. Is Bultmann's revival of the nineteenth-century interpretation of the resurrection as the rise of faith in the disciples adequate to explain the advent of the kerygma or the presence of the living word today?

6. One final point seems to bring to focus those already suggested. Bultmann insists that any doctrine concerning

Jesus Christ be defined not in terms of his "nature" but in terms of Christ's meaning "for me." Deobjectifying and demythologizing demand the rejection of the doctrine of the incarnation as traditionally interpreted in the Johannine and Pauline writings and the creeds of the church. The biblical passages especially must be reinterpreted in terms of the real scandal, that of God's activity, the living word, in the lives of men today. Although Bultmann renounces the knowledge of "Christ after the flesh," the church's kerygma proclaimed Christ "in the flesh." Thus there is a discontinuity, not only between the historical Jesus and the Christ-kerygma, but also between the original kerygma and the kerygma today. The problem arises whether Bultmann's devaluation of the incarnation, the historical Jesus, and historical facts does not constitute a docetism which transforms the Christian faith and its kerygma today into something radically different and discontinuous with the early church's kerygma concerning Jesus Christ. Put very simply, what is to prevent the complete separation of the kerygma today from any contact with the historical Jesus, the biblical testimonies to him, and the church's kerygma throughout the centuries? What ultimately keeps this existentialist kerygma Christian kerygma?

❖   ❖   ❖

It is apparent that both Kierkegaard and Bultmann have made major contributions to the discussion of the relationship of faith today to the historical Jesus and the New Testament documents concerning him. It is also quite apparent that the discussion is far from complete but must continue and presumably be revitalized in every new context and age of man's existence.

Notes

Part I

1. Albert Schweitzer, *The Quest of the Historical Jesus,* trans. W. Montgomery (New York: Macmillan, 1961), p. 10.

2. James M. Robinson., *A New Quest of the Historical Jesus* (London: S. C. M. Press, 1959, distributed in the U.S.A. by Allenson's Naperville, Ill.), p. 26.

3. Schweitzer, p. 3.

4. Hans Werner Baartsch, ed., *Kerygma and Myth,* I, trans. R. H. Fuller (New York: Harper and Brothers), 1961, p. 82.

5. Schweitzer, pp. 399-403.

6. Robinson, pp. 35-47.

7. Richard R. Niebuhr, *Resurrection and Historical Reason* (New York: Scribner's, 1957), pp. 23-24.

8. Paul S. Minear, and Morimoto, Paul S., *Kierkegaard and the Bible—an Index* (Princeton: Princeton Theological Seminary, 1953), p. 12.

9. Søren Kierkegaard, *Philosophical Fragments,* trans. D. Swenson, rev. trans. H. V. Hong (Princeton: Princeton University Press, 1962), title page.

10. Søren Kierkegaard, *Stages on Life's Way,* trans. W. Lowrie (Princeton: Princeton University Press, 1940), p. 218.

11. Søren Kierkegaard, *Thoughts on Crucial Situations,* trans. D. F. Swenson (Minneapolis: Augsburg, 1941), p. 38.

12. Søren Kierkegaard, *Repetition,* trans. W. Lowrie (Princeton: Princeton University Press, 1941), pp. 121-124.

13. Søren Kierkegaard, *Concluding Unscientific Postscript to the Philosophical Fragments,* trans. D. F. Swenson and W. Lowrie (Princeton: Princeton University Press, 1941), p. 321.

14. Søren Kierkegaard, *Works of Love,* trans. D. F. and L. M. Swenson (Princeton: Princeton University Press, 1946), pp. 79-80.

15. Søren Kierkegaard, *For Self-Examination,* trans. E. & H. Hong (Minneapolis: Augsburg, 1940), p. 25.

16. *Ibid.,* p. 29.

17. *Ibid.,* pp. 39, 50.

18. Søren Kierkegaard, *Training in Christianity,* trans. W. Lowrie (Princeton: Princeton University Press, 1941), p. 154.

19. Søren Kierkegaard, *The Sickness unto Death,* trans. W. Lowrie (Princeton: Princeton University Press, 1941), p. 3.

20. Søren Kierkegaard, *The Journals of Kierkegaard,* ed. and trans. A. Dru (London: Oxford University Press, 1938), p. 340.

21. Kierkegaard, *Training,* p. 79.

22. Kierkegaard, *Journals,* p. 338.

23. Kierkegaard, *Training,* p. 79.

24. Søren Kierkegaard, *Edifying Discourses,* III, trans. D. F. and L. M. Swenson (Minneapolis: Augsburg, 1943), p. 123.

25. Søren Kierkegaard, *Christian Discourses,* trans. W. Lowrie (New York: Oxford University Press, 1961), p. 228.

26. *Ibid.,* pp. 255-309.

27. Søren Kierkegaard, *Fear and Trembling,* trans. W. Lowrie (Princeton: Princeton University Press, 1945), p. 109.

28. Søren Kierkegaard, *Attack Upon Christendom,* trans. W. Lowrie (Princeton: Princeton University Press, 1944), p. 197.

29. Kierkegaard, *Journals,* p. 57.

30. *Sickness,* p. 11.

31. *Self-Examination,* p. 76.

32. *Ibid.*

33. *Ibid.,* p. 83.

34. *Ibid.*

35. *Training,* p. 27.

36. *Ibid.,* p. 14.

37. *Ibid.,* p. 9.

38. *Attack,* p. 108.

39. *Ibid.,* p. 109.

40. *Postscript,* p. 528.

41. *Ibid.,* p. 531.

42. *Ibid.,* p. 527.

43. *Ibid.,* p. 27.

44. *Ibid.,* p. 29.

45. *Self-Examination,* pp. 33-34.

46. Søren Kierkegaard, *On Authority and Revelation,* trans. W. Lowrie (Princeton: Princeton University Press, 1955), p. 27.

47. *Self-Examination,* p. 38.

48. *Fragments,* p. 11.

49. *Journals,* p. 15.

50. *Ibid.,* p. 167.

51. *Ibid.,* p. 59.

52. *Ibid.,* p. 238.

53. *Postscript,* p. 521.

54. *Ibid.,* p. 525.

55. *Training,* p. 89.

56. *Sickness,* p. 194.

57. *Attack,* p. 215.

58. *Training,* p. 38.

59. *Ibid.,* p. 59.

60. *Fear and Trembling,* p. 38.

61. *Ibid.,* p. 3.

62. Paul Tillich, *Theology of Culture* (New York: Oxford University Press, 1959), p. 82.

63. Niels Thulstrup, "Theological and Philosophical Studies of Kierkegaard in Scandinavia, 1945-1953," *Theology Today,* XII, p. 301. Used by permission.

64. *Fragments,* pp. 11-27.

65. *Ibid.,* title page.

66. *Ibid.,* p. 2.

67. *Postscript,* p. 3.

68. *Ibid.,* p. 14.

69. *Ibid.,* p. 20.

70. *Journals,* p. 319.

71. *Fragments,* pp. 46-67.

72. *Postscript,* pp. 101-106.

73. *Fragments,* p. 50.

74. *Postscript,* p. 108.

75. *Fragments,* p. 53.

76. *Postscript,* pp. 273-279.

77. *Ibid.,* p. 112.

78. *Fragments,* pp. 89-110.

79. *Ibid.,* p. 103.

80. *Postscript,* pp. 169-224.

81. *Ibid.,* p. 169.

82. *Fragments,* pp. 16-27.

83. *Fragments*, p. 18.
84. *Ibid.*, p. 32.
85. *Postscript*, p. 107.
86. *Fragments*, pp. 68-88.
87. *Ibid.*, p. 100.
88. *Ibid.*, p. 88.
89. *Ibid.*, p. 103.
90. *Ibid.*, pp. 66-71.
91. *Ibid.*, p. 82.
92. *Training*, p. 86.
93. *Ibid.*, pp. 40-60.
94. *Ibid.*, p. 98.
95. *Fragments*, pp. 111-138.
96. *Ibid.*, p. 87.
97. *Ibid.*
98. *Postscript*, p. 25.
99. *Ibid.*, p. 26.
100. *Ibid.*, p. 38.
101. *Fragments*, pp. 119-123.
102. *Ibid.*, p. 129.
103. *Postscript*, p. 49.
104. *Ibid.*, p. 25.
105. *Training*, p. 28.
106. *Sickness*, p. 207.
107. *Ibid.*, p. 192.
108. *Training*, p. 38.
109. *Ibid.*, p. 84.
110. *Postscript*, p. 512.
111. *Training*, p. 42.
112. *Fragments*, pp. 61-67.
113. *Ibid.*, p. 66.
114. *Ibid.*, p. 59.
115. *Ibid.*, p. 30.
116. *Postscript*, p. 57.
117. *Fragments*, pp. 73-76.
118. *Ibid.*, p. 133.
119. *Ibid.*, p. 80.
120. *Ibid.*, p. 74.
121. *Ibid.*, p. 22.
122. *Ibid.*, p. 87.
123. *Postscript*, p. 326.

124. *Fragments*, p. 130.
125. *Ibid.*, p. 131.
126. *Ibid.*, p. 134.
127. *Postscript*, p. 178.
128. *Fragments*, p. 129.
129. *Ibid.*
130. *Ibid.*, p. 127.
131. *Postscript*, p. 208.
132. *Ibid.*, p. 189.
133. *Fear and Trembling*, p. 36.
134. *Postscript*, p. 19.
135. *On Authority and Revelation*, p. 116.
136. Søren Kierkegaard, *The Concept of Dread*, trans. W. Lowrie (Princeton: Princeton University Press, 1944), p. 92.
137. *Authority*, p. 104.
138. *Postscript*, p. 32.
139. *Authority*, p. 59.
140. *Postscript*, p. 30.
141. *Ibid.*, p. 29.
142. *Ibid.*, p. 26.
143. *Training*, p. 98.
144. *Postscript*, p. 35.
145. *Ibid.*, pp. 25-42.
146. *Ibid.*, pp. 325-329, 340-341.
147. *Authority*, p. 109.
148. *Postscript*, pp. 45-47; *Training*, pp. 28-31; *Authority*, pp. 57-61.
149. *Training*, p. 29.
150. *Journals*, p. 322.
151. *Authority*, p. 114.
152. *Ibid.*, p. 110.
153. *Journals*, p. 192.
154. *Authority*, p. 109.
155. *Journals*, p. 352.
156. *Postscript*, p. 182.
157. *Training*, p. 147.
158. *Journals*, pp. 367-368.
159. *Authority*, p. 58.

Part II

1. Cf., Rudolf Bultmann, "The Primitive Christian Kerygma and the Historical Jesus," trans. C. E. Braaten & R. A. Harrisville, *The Historical Jesus and the Kerygmatic Christ* (New York: Abingdon, 1964), pp. 27-42.

2. Rudolf Bultmann, "The Case for Demythologizing: A Reply," trans. R. H. Fuller, *Kerygma and Myth*, II, ed. H. W. Bartsch (London: S.P.C.K., 1962), p. 192.

3. Rudolf Bultmann, "New Testament and Mythology," trans. R. H. Fuller, *Kerygma and Myth*, I, ed. H. W. Bartsch (New York: Harper & Brothers, 1961), p. 44.

4. Rudolf Bultmann, *Existence and Faith*, trans. S. M. Ogden (New York: Meridian Books, 1960), p. 28.

5. Rudolf Bultmann, *Essays, Philosophical and Theological*, trans. J. C. G. Grieg (London: SCM Press, 1955), p. 107.

6. Rudolf Bultmann, *Theology of the New Testament*, I, trans. K. Grobel (New York: Charles Scribner's Sons, 1954). p. 25.

7. "Bultmann Replies to his Critics," *Kerygma and Myth*, I, p. 197.

8. *Ibid.*, p. 198.

9. *Kerygma and Myth*, I, p. 14.

10. *Ibid.*, p. 108.

11. Rudolf Bultmann, *Jesus Christ and Mythology* (New York: Charles Scribner's Sons, 1958), p. 66.

12. *Ibid.*

13. *Theology*, I, p. 25.

14. *Kerygma and Myth*, I, pp. 196-7.

15. *Ibid.*, p. 198.

16. Cf., *Ibid.*, p. 199.

17. *Ibid.*, p. 196; *Jesus Christ*, pp. 68 f.

18. *Jesus Christ*, pp. 69-70.

19. *Kerygma and Myth*, I, p. 197.

20. *Ibid.*, p. 10, n. 2.

21. *Jesus Christ*, p. 43.

22. *Kerygma and Myth*, I, p. 4.

23. *Jesus Christ*, p. 37.

24. *Ibid.*, p. 18.

25. *Kerygma and Myth*, I, p. 16.

26. *Kerygma and Myth*, II, p. 183.

27. Rudolf Bultmann, *Theology of the New Testament*, II, trans. K. Grobel (New York: Charles Scribner's Sons, 1955), p. 240.

28. Cf., *Kerygma and Myth*, I, pp. 114-116.

29. *Jesus Christ*, p. 77.

30. *Existence*, p. 86.

31. *Jesus Christ*, p. 73.

32. Rudolf Bultmann, *The Presence of Eternity—History and Eschatology* (New York: Harper & Brothers, 1957), p. 155.

33. Rudolf Bultmann, *Jesus and the Word*, trans. L. P. Smith and E. H. Lantero (New York: Charles Scribner's Sons, 1958), pp. 13-14.

34. *Historical Jesus*, p. 20.

35. Cf., Theology, I, p. 3; also Rudolf Bultmann, *History of the Synoptic Tradition*, trans. J. Marsh (Oxford: Basil Blackwell, 1963).

36. *Jesus*, pp. 12-13.

37. Cf., *Theology*, I, pp. 3-32.

38. *Existence*, p. 52.

39. Cf., *Historical Jesus*, pp. 22-23.

40. *Ibid.*, p. 23.

41. *Theology*, I, p. 33.

42. *Synoptic Tradition*, p. 374.

43. *Historical Jesus*, p. 16.

44. James M. Robinson, *op. cit.*, pp. 36-47.

45. *Historical Jesus*, pp. 25-26.

46. *Theology*, II, p. 251.

47. *Jesus*, pp. 3-4, 10.

48. *Essays*, p. 256.

49. *Existence*, p. 294.

50. *Kerygma and Myth*, II, p. 187.

51. *Presence of Eternity*, p. 152.

52. *Kerygma and Myth*, I, p. 207.

53. *Theology*, I, p. 33.

54. *Jesus Christ*, pp. 81-82.

55. *Jesus*, p. 214.

56. *Ibid.*, p. 213.

57. *Kerygma and Myth*, I, pp. 36-38.

58. *Ibid.*, p. 39.

59. *Ibid.*

60. *Ibid.*, p. 43.

61. *Ibid.*, p. 112.

62. *Ibid.*, pp. 41-42.

63. Cf., *Theology*, I, pp. 187-188.

64. *Ibid.*, p. 31.

65. *Ibid.*, p. 26.

66. *Ibid.*, p. 30.

67. *Essays*, p. 287.

68. *Kerygma and Myth*, I, p. 117.

69. *Ibid.*, p. 44.

70. *Ibid.*

71. *Ibid.*, p. 117.

72. *Historical Jesus*, p. 42.

73. Richard R. Niebuhr, *op. cit.*

Bibliography

Baartsch, Hans Werner, ed. *Kerygma and Myth*, Vol. I, trans. R. H. Fuller. New York: Harper and Brothers, Torchbooks, 1961.

————*Kerygma and Myth*, Vol. II, trans. R. H. Fuller. London: S.P.C.K., 1962.

Braaten, Carl E., and Harrisville, Roy A., ed. and trans., *The Historical Jesus and the Kerygmatic Christ*. New York: Abingdon, 1964.

Bultmann, Rudolf, *Essays, Philosophical and Theological*, trans. J. C. G. Grieg. London: SCM Press Ltd., 1955.

————*Existence and Faith*, ed. and trans. S. M. Ogden. New York: Meridian Books, Inc. (Living Age Books), 1960.

————*The History of the Synoptic Tradition*, trans. J. Marsh. Oxford: Basil Blackwell, 1963.

————*Jesus and the Word*, trans. L. P. Smith and E. H. Lantero. New York: Charles Scribner's Sons, 1958.

————*Jesus Christ and Mythology*. New York: Charles Scribner's Sons, 1958.

————*Primitive Christianity in Its Contemporary Setting*, trans. R. H. Fuller. New York: Meridian Books, Inc. (Living Age Books), 1956.

————*The Presence of Eternity, History and Eschatology*. New York: Harper and Brothers, 1957.

————*Theology of the New Testament*, Vol. I, trans. K. Grobel. New York: Charles Scribner's Sons, 1954.

————*Theology of the New Testament*, Vol. II, trans. K. Grobel. New York: Charles Scribner's Sons, 1955.

Kierkegaard, Søren, *Attack upon Christendom*, trans. W. Lowrie. Princeton: Princeton University Press, 1944.

————*Christian Discourses*, trans. W. Lowrie. New York: Oxford University Press (Galaxy Book), 1961.

————*The Concept of Dread*, trans. W. Lowrie. Princeton: Princeton University Press, 1944.

————*Concluding Unscientific Postscript to the Philosophical Fragments*, trans. D. F. Swenson and W. Lowrie. Princeton: Princeton University Press, 1941.

99

————Edifying Discourses, Vol. III, trans. D. F. & L. M. Swenson. Minneapolis: Augsburg, 1943.

————Fear and Trembling, trans. W. Lowrie. Princeton: Princeton University Press, 1945.

————For Self-Examination, trans. E. & H. Hong. Minneapolis: Augsburg, 1940.

————The Journals of Kierkegaard, trans. & ed. A. Dru. London: Oxford University Press, 1938.

————On Authority and Revelation, trans. W. Lowrie. Princeton: Princeton University Press, 1955.

————Philosophical Fragments, trans. D. Swenson, rev. trans. H. V. Hong. Princeton: Princeton University Press, 1962.

————Repetition, trans. W. Lowrie. Princeton: Princeton University Press, 1941.

————The Sickness unto Death, trans. W. Lowrie. Princeton: Princeton University Press, 1941.

————Stages on Life's Way, trans. W. Lowrie. Princeton: Princeton University Press, 1940.

————Thoughts on Crucial Situations, trans. D. F. Swenson. Minneapolis: Augsburg, 1941.

————Training in Christianity, trans. W. Lowrie. Princeton: Princeton University Press, 1941.

————Works of Love, trans. D. F. & L. M. Swenson. Princeton: Princeton University Press, 1946.

Minear, Paul S., and Morimoto, Paul S., Kierkegaard and the Bible—An Index. Princeton: Princeton Theological Seminary, 1953.

Niebuhr, Richard R., Resurrection and Historical Reason. New York: Charles Scribner's Sons, 1957.

Robinson, James M., A Quest of the Historical Jesus. London: S. C. M. Press, 1959. Distributed in the U.S.A. by Allenson's, Naperville, Ill.

Schweitzer, Albert, The Quest of the Historical Jesus, trans. W. Montgomery. New York: Macmillan, 1961.

Thulstrup, Niels, "Theological and Philosophical Studies of Kierkegaard in Scandinavia, 1945-1953." Theology Today, XII.

Tillich, Paul, Theology of Culture. New York: Oxford University Press, 1959.

The Author

Herbert C. Wolf is associate professor of religion at Wittenberg University, Springfield, Ohio. Previously he served as the National Lutheran Council campus pastor at Michigan State University, taught in the University religion department, and was pastor of University Lutheran Church, East Lansing, Mich. He also has been an instructor in religion at Capital University, Columbus, Ohio.

He has published articles in the *Journal of Bible and Religion* and the *Lutheran Quarterly*, as well as in church-related publications.

Prof. Wolf has degrees from Johns Hopkins University, Baltimore, Md., the Evangelical Lutheran Theological Seminary, Columbus, Ohio, and the University of Chicago. He has twice been the recipient of a Danforth Teacher Study Grant for study at Harvard University.